LATRINAE ET FORICAE

LATRINAE ET FORICAE

Toilets in the Roman World

Barry Hobson

Duckworth

This impression 2010
First published in 2009 by
Gerald Duckworth & Co. Ltd.
90-93 Cowcross Street, London EC1M 6BF
Tel: 020 7490 7300
Fax: 020 7490 0080
info@duckworth-publishers.co.uk
www.ducknet.co.uk

A catalogue record for this book is available
from the British Library

ISBN 978 0 7156 3850 7

Typeset by Ray Davies
Printed and bound in UK by
CPI Antony Rowe, Chippenham and Eastbourne

Contents

Acknowledgements

I wish to acknowledge a great debt to the many people who have helped in the production of this book. First, to the combined efforts of a large number of people associated with the Anglo-American Project in Pompeii (AAPP), especially the Directors, Rick Jones and Damian Robinson, and the environmental specialists Jill Thompson and Andrew Jones. Many thanks are also due to those supervisors whose reports have contributed to my research. They include Michael Anderson, Darren Bailey, Els Coppens, Megan Dennis, Briece Edwards, Steven Ellis, Diane Fortenberry, Jason Urbanus and Claire Weiss. Also Jennifer Wehby, Shellie McKinley, Jessica Self, Helen Ackers, Cettina Lagana, Graham Miles-Turner, Roy Andrews, Natalie Pitcher and the many other students over the years whose enthusiasm has been a source of amazement and encouragement. Special thanks must go to Helen Molesworth, David Rider, Emily Schurr, and Kate and Sue Trusler. Without the assistance given to me by these five helpers I would never have been able to survey what has amounted to almost the whole of the city of Pompeii. Appreciation must also be expressed to the Soprintendenza of Pompeii and staff for permission to carry out research and to the *custodi* who gave me access to parts of the city that are not usually open to public view.

For academic background I have frequently drawn on articles published in Italian, for the translation of which I am indebted to Pamela Cooksey. Similarly I am indebted to Paul Pascal of Washington University, Seattle, for his help with Latin translations.

Other people must be thanked for their generous cooperation; these include Gemma Jansen (whose article on latrines in *Sequence and Space in Pompeii* was the first I read on the subject), Adam Goldwater and Natalie De Haan, all of whom have brought new aspects of Roman latrines to my notice.

The AAPP is to be thanked for allowing the reproduction of a number of photographs, and I am also extremely grateful to a number of organisations who have given me permission to publish photographs of latrines. These include English Heritage for Chesters Fort (Fig. 54), the National Trust for Housesteads Fort (Figs 44, 47) and Chedworth Villa (Fig. 57), Newport Museum for Prysg Field Barracks (Fig. 50), Tyne and Wear Museum Services for pictures from Segedunum Roman Fort, Baths and Museum (Figs 48, 55) and from Arbeia Roman Fort and Museum (Figs 46, 56). I would also like to thank the Vindolanda Trust for permission to publish my Vindolanda pictures (Figs 51, 52, 53), the Getty Museum (Fig. 134) and the Berlin Museum (Fig. 137).

A number of my friends have provided me with photographs for this publication: Kate Trusler (Fig. 13), Michael Lindley (Figs 21, 22, 109), Helen Molesworth (Figs 24, 31), Paul Garthwaite (Figs 25, 26, 27), Brian Howcroft (Fig. 35), and Margaret Hinchliffe (Fig. 54); without them the visual impact of Roman latrines throughout the Mediterranean would be much reduced.

Special thanks must go to the British Museum for permission to use the photograph of the chariot latrine as the cover of this book and also to Dr Bruce Campbell for permission to use the plan of Prysg Field Barracks latrine, Caerleon (Fig. 49).

I would like to add grateful thanks to Deborah Blake and all the staff at Duckworth Publishers for their help and patience during the editing period of this book. Any errors are mine alone

Finally, I wish to thank my friends Malcolm Haigh for editorial help and Arthur Stephens for stimulating my enthusiasm for latrines when we excavated in VI.1.1 in 2002.

Preface

Why, you may ask, a book on Roman toilets? Is anybody interested in this rather esoteric subject?

Toilets do appear to have a degree of common appeal, probably because it is a subject about which everybody has a degree of expert personal knowledge and experience. My original medical career has given me some insights into the subjects of hygiene and disease. This knowledge was further stimulated by Andrew Jones and his work on intestinal parasites in faecal material. Time spent with Rick Jones and Damian Robinson in Pompeii introduced me to the distribution of latrines in the community and their situation within individual buildings, along with giving me some perception of the development of the provision of facilities over time, especially the use of water for drainage and cleansing.

These basic data stimulated questions about Roman concepts of privacy and then wider issues of usage. Perhaps the rich did not use these latrines because of the smell, and so they were inevitably the domain of the lower classes, who decorated them with appropriate graffiti?

The use of human excrement as a fertiliser is well known. Perhaps less well studied is the part this played in the overall disposal of rubbish. Modern urban society has a problem with this. Did the Romans also?

Guides to Roman sites occasionally indicate the location of individual latrines, but it is safe to say that overviews of the subject are rare. This book explores the wide archaeological occurrence of these facilities and investigates the known historical facts and the literature of the time in order to draw conclusions about social attitudes and behaviour.

The Latin words in the title are used in an attempt to differentiate between *foricae* or multi-seat public toilets and *latrinae* or single-seat private toilets. This differentiation is not absolutely clear-cut, since sometimes there are single-seat public toilets and sometimes two, three, or even more seats in private toilets. As will become obvious in the book, up to now descriptions of house latrines have been much less common than records of large public toilets. An attempt has been made to rectify this.

In the discussion of this subject it is hard to avoid the use of terminology which might be offensive to some. There are aspects of the study of human excrement which may give rise to disgust. This is partly to do with the cultural taboos; partly to do with the language used to express aspects of behaviour associated with excretion. Scatological words occur occasionally, mostly when quoting other authors' translations. It is hoped that the diversity of the issues explored will compensate and that the reader will, when visiting Roman sites, be prepared to look at the latrines with a new understanding of this particular aspect of Roman life.

Throughout the book BCE (Before Common Era) and CE (Common Era) and are used in place of BC and AD.

Toilets in the Roman world: an introduction

What do visitors look for when they visit ancient Roman sites? Is it perhaps the mosaics, the wall decoration, the splendid architecture? There is nothing more stirring to the imagination than Roman amphitheatres such as the Colosseum in Rome or the fine example at El Djem in Tunisia (Fig. 1), where you can almost see the gladiators in the arena. From the top row of the theatre at Ephesus the wonderful acoustics mean that you can clearly hear a conversation on the stage. Resting on a bench in the Pantheon and marvelling at the construction of the dome, you realise what talented engineers the Romans were.

Archaeology and ancient history can seem to emphasise the monumental and the heroic while passing over the daily life of the ordinary people. The only historical event relating to Roman toilets is that in 222 CE the Emperor Elagabalus was murdered by the Praetorian Guard while in a latrine (*Scriptores Historiae Augustae* II.17.1). Tourists at ancient sites

1. Amphitheatre at El Djem.

may occasionally notice a Roman toilet, but it is highly likely that they will pass it by.

It might be reasonable to suppose that, since emptying the bowels is an everyday necessity and there are between 200 and 300 domestic toilets in Pompeii, there must be huge numbers elsewhere. The evidence is sketchy, however, and the study of this integral part of Roman life has been relatively neglected. On the other hand, there are toilets at many sites if one knows where to look, and what to look for.

Rome, Ostia and Hadrian's Villa

In any discussion of Roman latrines it is appropriate to start in Rome. A city with a population of between one and two million people must have required some way of dealing with excrement. What evidence is there for toilets? Was there a drainage system to remove the material? Regrettably very few ancient toilets survive in Rome itself and it can be hard to get permission to see those that do. One visible to passers-by is in the Largo Argentina. This site is famous for its three temples and a modern stone which marks the spot where Julius Caesar was assassinated. The latrine here is a long multi-seater with a well defined gutter and a remnant of stone seating at one end (Fig. 2). Another multi-seat latrine exists in the Via Garibaldi. It is extremely difficult to get permission to see it, but as Fig. 3 shows it has well preserved decorated wall plaster.

Ancient domestic toilets are not obvious in Rome today, although there is some written excavation evidence that there were a good many of these, which apparently did not exit into sewers.

The most famous Roman drain is the Cloaca Maxima, originally constructed around 600 BCE to drain the marshes around the forum by order of the King of Rome, Tarquin the Proud. Special permission is needed to descend into this marvel of Roman engineering. Walking in pitch darkness, ankle-deep in water, with the odd rat running past you, is quite an experience. The present condition of the drain after 2,500 years of existence is a tribute to the engineers who built it. The cloaca proper seems to have begun near the north-west corner of the Forum of Augustus. From this point to the Via Alessandrina it is built entirely of *peperino* (a kind of volcanic stone), vaulted, and paved with blocks of lava – the characteristic style of the Republic; while onwards as far as the forum the roof has been restored in brick-faced concrete of the imperial period. The channel is here 4.20 m high and 3.20 m wide. Eight branches empty into this section – none of them, as Lanciani (1873) notes, from private houses, which must have relied largely on cesspools.

Two amazing sites, Ostia and Hadrian's Villa at Tivoli, are within easy reach of Rome. Although very different in nature, Ostia being a town, while the villa is a palace estate, they both offer a fine selection of latrines.

Among a number of latrines in Ostia are the following: V.ii.4-5, House

2. Latrine in the Largo Argentina, Rome.

3. Latrine in the Via Garibaldi, Rome.

4. Latrine in the House of Fortuna Annonaria, Ostia, V.ii.8.

5. The forum latrine I.xii.1 at Ostia.

4

of the Porch, a two-seater on the ground floor below the staircase; V.ii.6-7, in front of the entrance to the Baths of the Philosopher with ten to fifteen seats; V.ii.8, House of Fortuna Annonaria, a lavish one-seater below the staircase (Fig. 4); V.ii.13, House of the Well, a one-seater below the staircase in the south-east corner of the house (Boersma 1996). The Barracks of the Vigiles has a large multi-seat latrine and near the forum is another which appears to have been converted from two shops (Fig. 5). The doorways indicate that there may have been revolving doors.

There are a considerable number of multi-seat latrines in Ostia, giving the impression that they were generally the only option. Perhaps this also applied in Rome where, in the fourth century CE, there are said to have been 144 *foricae*.

Occasionally a single domestic latrine has been found, as shown in Fig. 6. Five of these are situated under staircases (*subscalaria*) (I.vi.1; I.vii.1; I.xi.2; I.xii.2; I.xii.3). The seats are made from slabs of white marble (certainly used second-hand), as are the walls, the small fountain on the

6. Single-seat latrine in house adjacent to the House of the Round Temple, Ostia.

7. Latrine in the Tavern of Fortunatus, Ostia, II.vi.1.

8. Latrine in the School of Trajan, Ostia, IV.v.15.

corner and the pavement. The latrine dates back to the second century CE, being contemporary with the building. Another domestic toilet, possibly a two-seater, can be seen in the Tavern of Fortunatus (Fig. 7). This one has a large water tank next to it with an obvious feeder pipe and an exit pipe to enable the tiles in the latrine to be flushed. It is highly likely that the water from such a large tank also served other needs within the tavern. The latrine in the School of Trajan has four seats, with marble behind, some of which is reconstruction (Fig. 8).

Hadrian's Villa, situated about 30 km from Rome, is a huge estate covering 120 hectares. Its many buildings have revealed a possible forty-seven toilets, nineteen of which were for one person and ten multi-seaters, one of which is circular. The multi-seat latrine in the Hall of Cubicles is shown in Fig. 9. In the analysis of these latrines there is a good argument for them having been designed for people of differing social class. 'The emperor and his guests had single-seaters, while in the baths they used multi-seaters. The staff had only multi-seaters at their disposal' (Jansen 2003). In one of the multi-seaters there are partitions, the only example of this that we know of from the Roman world. This introduces aspects of privacy to which we will turn later. In the peristyle pool building the single-seat latrine is situated in a very pleasant curved niche. There is a scar in the floor where a pipe brought in water for flushing (Fig. 10). A single-seat latrine in the Scenic Triclinium has a nice floor of *opus sectile* and also the remains of marble seating (Fig. 11).

9. Multi-seat latrine in the Hall of Cubicles, Hadrian's Villa.

10. Niche latrine, Hadrian's Villa.

11. Latrine in the Scenic Triclinium, Hadrian's Villa.

South Italy and Sicily

South of Rome lies the Bay of Naples. Here there are a number of sites with latrines dating to the Roman period.

Cumae, lying to the north of the Bay of Naples, has a long history of occupation lasting over a thousand years. Despite this, the hill site, which as well as two temples houses the Cave of the Sibyl, has only one latrine and this is in a most exposed site. There is no obvious pit, and a bucket may have been used to dispose of the excreta (Fig. 12).

Within the Bay of Naples to the south of Cumae was Baia, one of the most pleasant places for wealthy Romans to spend their free time. As a result of seismic movement much of the town now lies under water and what remains does not have many latrines. The one shown here (Fig. 13) is within the so-called Baths of the Temple of Venus.

To the east of Baia on the Bay of Naples lies Pozzuoli, in Roman times Puteoli. Originally a Greek settlement, Dicearchia, it became a Roman *colonia* in 194 BCE. Famous for its Flavian amphitheatre, it also boasts a *macellum* (market) known as the Temple of Serapis. Here Andrea de Jorio

12. Latrine at Cumae.

9

13. Latrine at Baia.

(1769-1851), Canon of the Cathedral of Naples and an archaeologist, excavated two multi-seat latrines which he euphemistically described as 'bath suites'. Figs 14 and 15 show the pedestals for the seats. The water channels in both are well preserved, as is the floor of the eastern one.

Although only a few kilometres from Pompeii, the town of Herculaneum is different in many ways, not least in the distribution of toilets. Hardly any are visible in the houses and the only multi-seat latrine supplies the men's baths (Fig. 16).

To the rear of the House of the Grand Portal, lying under the stairs, is a single-seat domestic toilet (Fig. 17). Two pedestals define where the wooden seat was laid, and there is a foot-rest stone in front. What might appear at first glance to be a water tank is in fact the flushing floor which passes beneath the foot-rest.

Pipes coming from upper storey latrines do exist in Herculaneum (Fig. 18). However, in contrast to Pompeii where almost all toilets drain into cesspits, here they appear to drain into sewers which run under Cardo V towards the sea.

Just outside the walls of Pompeii lies the Villa of the Mysteries, famous for its enigmatic frescos. The latrine illustrated (Fig. 19) is not of comparable splendour.

The Villa of Oplontis, situated by the Bay of Naples between Pompeii

14. Eastern latrine in the *macellum*, Pozzuoli.

15. Western latrine in the *macellum*, Pozzuoli.

16. Multi-seat latrine
in the men's baths,
Herculaneum.

17. Latrine in the
House of the Grand
Portal, Herculaneum.

18. Pipe from upper
storey latrine,
Herculaneum.

and Herculaneum, is a palatial property which is thought to have been owned by Poppaea, wife of Nero. Here, in contrast to the Villa of the Mysteries, can be seen a latrine room with a water channel in front of the seating area (Fig. 20). This channel was fed from a large water cistern on the right, the water passing around the channel to its far end and then descending into the sewer. This feature is common and its significance will be discussed later (see pp. 123-8).

The latrines of this palace and those of Hadrian's Villa are not unique. The magnificent Villa del Casale in Piazza Armerina, Sicily, has sixty-three rooms and three latrines. It may have been built for the Emperor Maximian (286-310 CE) as a hunting lodge, but other owners have been postulated. Its mosaics, measuring in total 3,500 square metres and making use of thirty million *tesserae*, are among the most magnificent in the Roman world. The latrines vary in size and shape from the large semicircular one between the atrium and the bath suite (Fig. 21) to a smaller 'private' one which probably had ten seats (Fig. 22). There is a feeder tank for the water to the right of the entrance. The mosaic flooring of the latrine portrays animals, in particular a horse and a leopard. The third

19. Latrine in the Villa of the Mysteries.

20. Latrine in the Villa of Oplontis.

21. Semicircular latrine in the Villa del Casale, Sicily.

22. 'Private' latrine in the Villa del Casale.

and smallest latrine is on the opposite side of the villa near the great basilica.

Semicircular latrines are by no means rare in the Roman world. Examples can be found as far apart as Piercebridge in Yorkshire and Thuburbo Majus in Tunisia.

The Empire

By the beginning of the second century CE the Roman Empire was approaching its zenith. Monumental building was taking place in new cities, particularly in North Africa. If we are to appreciate the height of luxury in Roman buildings, perhaps this is the place to look for perfection in their latrines. In general latrines are not hard to find, and there are many Roman sites in North Africa, from Morocco and Algeria (Mauretania) through Tunisia and Libya (Tripolitania and the Pentapolis) to Egypt, in which to look. Almost all the famous cities have large multi-seat latrines which are well worth examination. Occasionally toilet seats are found that are clearly not in their original position (Fig. 23)

So far the sites discussed have all been in Italy and Sicily. The Roman Empire, of course, embraced Europe as far north as the Antonine Wall, and to the south across the Mediterranean into North Africa. From Spain in the west to Turkey, Syria and Jordan, Roman sites abound. Searching the web for Roman latrines produces pictures of places as far apart as Philippi (www.bibleplaces.com), Hechingen-Stein (www.villa-rustica.de/indexe.html) and Leptis Magna (www.galenfrysinger.com/leptis_baths_libya.htm). The first of these is noteworthy because it is a religious site, the second is a museum and the third has stimulated many tourist photographs.

23. Toilet seat leaning against a wall at Bulla Regia, Tunis.

24. Latrine in the Agora, Athens.

Roman influence extended over a number of centuries in Western Europe, so it is quite reasonable to expect sites of Roman occupation to have latrines. The development of Roman influence in Greece is indicated by the latrine in the Agora in Athens (Fig. 24).

The ruins at Vaison la Romaine form the largest archaeological site in France. A number of the houses contain latrines – the Maison au Dauphin boasts one that would have seated a large number of people (Goudineau 1979) (Fig. 25). The seating is no longer present and may have been wooden. The Maison du Buste en Argent has a small room seating eight people with a doorway off a corridor (Fig. 26). In this case the seating is of stone. In a third house, the Maison la Tonelle, is yet another latrine also with stone seating (Fig. 27).

A toilet at Vilamoura in Portugal (Fig. 28) lies at the base of a watchtower (part of a large villa complex) overlooking a lagoon, the mooring place for Roman ships.

Merida, in modern Spain, was founded as Augusta Emerita by the Emperor Augustus in 25 BCE and became the capital of Roman Lusitania. As well as the latrine illustrated here (Fig. 29) it has a theatre, an amphitheatre and a circus, along with temples and an aqueduct.

During the first century BCE Rome was expanding to the east. In 64 BCE Pompey effectively ended the Seleucid Empire and Antioch was made

25. Latrine in the Maison au Dauphin, Vaison la Romaine.

26. Latrine in the Maison du Buste en Argent, Vaison la Romaine.

27. Latrine in the Maison la Tonelle, Vaison la Romaine.

28. Latrine in Vilamoura, Portugal.

29. Latrine in Merida, Spain.

capital of the new Roman Province of Syria. This provided a buffer against the military expansion of Parthia but offered trade routes from east to west and vice versa.

Romanisation brought changes to this area, and a study of the water supply and its links to latrines is brilliantly covered in a doctoral thesis by Zena Kamash (Kamash 2006). This describes 22 public latrines in the Near East. Not a great many! Fifteen of them were associated with bath houses, and most were dated to the fourth century CE. Judaea has relatively few, and this suggests that cultural beliefs in that area led to less willingness to accept Roman toilet and bathing behaviours because of the shame of nakedness and the Jewish law relating to disposal of faecal material.

In Syria, Apamea has a latrine in an *impluvium* style reflecting the openness of the multi-seat toilets in North Africa (Fig. 30).

A notable latrine is to be found in Palmyra. Modern appreciation of this city dates from 1691 when a small band of British merchants recorded inscriptions and descriptions of the site. Dr Halifax, one of the visitors, commented on seeing the Baths of Diocletion: 'in these ruins we found ye only latrine' (Halifax 1695).

Archaeological excavation of private houses in this part of the Roman Empire is very meagre, and those which have been recorded are almost all of high status. This makes it difficult to comment upon the prevalence of

30. Latrine in the forum, Apamea, Syria.

domestic latrines. The Palace of the Dux Ripae at Dura Europos (third century CE) has a bathhouse with its own latrine as well as a small latrine in the house itself.

Jerash (Gerasa), situated in a fertile valley in the Hills of Gilead, is probably the most excavated of the cities of the Decapolis. These were Hellenistic in origin and developed during the first and second centuries CE into large metropolises with fine civic and religious buildings. In 106 CE the Emperor Trajan created the province of Arabia to which he annexed the Nabatean Empire and the Decapolis. Trade via the new roads built by the Romans, including the Via Nova route from Aqaba to Damascus, brought real wealth to the area, and an inscription on the North Gate refers to Trajan as 'saviour and founder'.

The Baths of Placcus at Jerash were built by a bishop of that name in 454/5 CE (Browning 1982: 186). The latrine here may well be considered to reflect Byzantine, rather than Roman, culture.

In Turkey in the city of Ephesus there are eighteen latrines. The study of these has recently been expanded by Gemma Jansen who notes that eight of them have accommodation for from twelve to sixty persons. Nine of the remainder have between two and eight seats and only one house has a single-seat latrine. Some of these latrines are dated to the late antique period (fourth to seventh centuries CE). They are particularly noteworthy

21

for their paintings and inscriptions, the one in the philosophers' latrine telling the users to take regular bowel movements seriously. At Side, also in Turkey, there is a single latrine visible to the modern visitor, though there were almost certainly more in antiquity.

By the end of the first century CE North Africa had become rich as a result of the export of grain, olives and other commodities to Rome. In Volubilis, a major Roman city in Morocco, the one multi-seat latrine is not well preserved but the stone floor gives an indication of the quality of its construction (Fig. 31).

Currently Algeria is not easy to visit, but its ancient sites are remarkable. The Roman colony of Thamagudi (now Timgad) was founded by the Emperor Trajan in 100 CE to house retired legionaries. The main part of the town is geometric. There is a theatre within the city and two large baths outside, one to the north and the other to the south. At Timgad there are a number of latrines, including two single-seat toilets just off the forum and latrines associated with the Thermes des Filadelfes, the Petits Thermes Nord-Est and the Thermes dits Du Marché de Sertius. The house known as the Maison de Confidius has a five-seat latrine in the south-east corner to the right of the entrance (Ballu 1911).

31. Latrine in Volubilis, Morocco.

32. Latrine in the Baths of the Cyclops, Dougga, Tunisia.

Dougga is the largest Roman site in Tunisia. Originally a Punic town, it allied itself with Rome and became a *colonia* by the end of the second century CE. Fig. 32 shows the the latrine associated with the Baths of the Cyclops, part of the House of Trifolium which is said to have been a brothel. Dr James Berry, travelling with two ladies, described this latrine in a medical journal (Berry 1921). It is typical of latrines of the period, with stone seats beneath which there was a deep drain with running water. In front of the seats runs a gutter which carried fresh water from a nearby cistern. This water passed out through the wall of the latrine building, falling directly onto the stones below and contributing to the cleansing of the street.

A magnificent arch to the Emperor Diocletian marks the southern boundary of Sbeitla (Sufetula) in Tunisia, but even more impressive is the triad of temples to Minerva, Jupiter and Juno (Fig. 33). Sufetula was probably founded in the second century CE; by the third century it was a major producer of olive oil and had become an important economic centre. In the baths to the north of the Church of St Vitalis is a small multi-seat latrine. There is little evidence of masonry supports for the seats, which are missing (Fig. 34). There are two large bath complexes at Thuburbo Majus. The latrine in the Summer Baths is semicircular but is not well preserved. However, the latrine of the Winter Baths shows the fresh water

33. Temples to Minerva, Jupiter and Juno in Sbeitla, Tunisia.

34. Latrine in the baths in Sbeitla.

35. Latrine in the Winter Baths, Thuburbo Majus.

gutter and the paved central area, although the seating arrangements are again missing (Fig. 35).

As in modern times, so in the ancient world there were different types of toilets in different situations. In the Roman cities of North Africa the domestic variety of toilet is rare and might be a single stone seat, as one found at Dougga, or occasionally a two-seater, as in the House of the Hunt at Bulla Regia. Originally the capital of one of three small Roman kingdoms in Numidia (now Tunisia), Bulla Regia became prosperous during the reign of Hadrian. A large proportion of each property was built underground, giving ideal conditions in the winter, which could be very cold, and a retreat in the summer if the weather was too hot. Latrines do not appear to have been sited in these subterranean rooms. On the ground floor of the House of the Hunt there is a double latrine (Fig. 36). The floor of the room is decorated with a simple mosaic and at the base of the stone front there is a drainage hole which would have allowed water to flush the mosaic and enter the drainage of the latrine. The seat is of thick stone, which is replicated in a single-seat toilet in another house.

With its natural harbour, Sabratha (in modern Libya) began as a settlement for the Carthaginian coastal trade of the southern Mediterranean. It became one of the three cities of Tripolitana along with

36. Two-seat latrine in the House of the Hunt, Bulla Regia, Tunisia.

Leptis Magna and Oea (Tripoli). Commonly, Roman bath houses included toilet facilities. As is the case with almost all large Roman towns, it has an amphitheatre, temples and public baths. The latrine in the Seaward Baths has marble seating, with the water gutter running in front of the seats (Fig. 37). In a Roman villa adjacent to the site there is a small latrine with a mosaic floor (Fig. 38). The water gutter here is constructed with mosaic *tesserae* in what is called a *guilloche* pattern (Field 1998). This degree of opulence indicates the wealth accrued from exporting grain, olive oil and other commodities across the Mediterranean to Rome.

Leptis Magna started as a Phoenician trading port. From the sixth century BCE it was under Carthaginian administration, joining Rome in 111 BCE and becoming a *colonia* under the Emperor Trajan. Most of the buildings date from the reign of the Emperor Septimius Severus (193-211 CE) who was born in the city.

The huge bath house, dedicated to the Emperor Hadrian, has two large latrines (Figs 39 & 40), one allegedly for women which is slightly smaller than the one for the men. Each has a central peristyle with a colonnade, within which are seats in rows down three of the four sides. The side opposite the entrances in the men's latrine is 16 m long and the other two sides are over 13 m, giving a seating capacity of about forty-eight persons.

37. Latrine in the Seaward Baths, Sabratha, Libya.

38. Mosaic water gutter in the villa at Sabratha.

The diameter of each hole is only 15.5 cm and they are between 60 and 65 cm apart. The seating is of marble, 8 cm thick. The expense of importing this material meant that great care had to taken when cutting out the holes for the seats. Seemingly someone erred when marking out the marble on the eastern side of the men's latrine prior to cutting the seat holes, for there is an obvious outline which has mistakenly been made for the positioning of such a hole (Fig. 41). The drainage channel beneath the seats is 1.35 m deep at its entrance and falls to a depth of 2 m at its exit. In the women's latrine the holes are only 20 cm apart but the hole diameter is 20 cm. Here the drain falls 13 cm round the three sides where there were over forty seats. Roman authors tell us that social intercourse took place within these establishments, but little is known about who used them. This will be discussed in some detail in Chapter 10.

These latrines are of considerable architectural interest and have been catalogued in an extraordinary book by Richard Neudecker (*Die Pracht der Latrine*, 1994). Their sheer size and magnificence makes one eager to suppose that this was repeated all along the North African coast. However, although there are multi-seat latrines in Ptolemais, Cyrene and Sbeitla they are relatively small, which leads one to ask, if these were the only facilities for a population of several thousand persons, what other options were there?

39. 'Women's latrine', Hadrianic baths, Leptis Magna, Libya.

40. 'Men's latrine', Hadrianic baths, Leptis Magna.

41. Marking error on marble seating, Hadrianic baths, Leptis Magna.

Tolmeita (Ptolemais), east of Leptis Magna, first came into existence in the sixth century BCE, but its foundation as a city was accomplished by one of the Hellenistic kings of Egypt, who gave it this name and laid out streets and public buildings. The king was probably Ptolemy III Euergetes. The only recordable latrine is in the baths. It is very overgrown and uncared for.

Old Roman cities are fairly well represented all over North Africa, but it is difficult to find any better site for Greek and Roman ruins than Cyrene. Set back from the sea, the city tumbles down the hillside with views across the coastal plain to Apollonia and the sea. Despite the size of the city and its remarkable Temple to Zeus (Fig. 43), the only latrine is a small six-seater attached to the Great Baths (Fig. 42).

Although this apparent absence of domestic toilets in North Africa may indicate a preference for public latrines or a cultural indifference to domestic facilities, it may also reflect the unimportance of toilets to nineteenth- and twentieth-century archaeologists, who concentrated on

42. Latrine in the Great Baths, Cyrene, Libya.

43. Temple of Zeus, Cyrene.

excavating and restoring large monuments and seldom attempted to investigate the lives of ordinary people. Examining the incidence of latrines in other parts of the Roman Empire may help to resolve this question.

*

Despite the apparent plethora of available material outlined above, not a great deal is known about Roman toilets. This may be because the discussion of toilets elicits a variety of responses, ranging from hearty laughter to positive distaste. To quote a recent author, 'the subject is unglamorous' (Wilson 2000: 151). There may be a reluctance to discuss a subject in which some of the vocabulary is objectionable.

It certainly appears that cultural influences relating to vulgarity, especially during the mid-nineteenth to mid-twentieth century, had a great deal to do with the lack of research into this subject. Perhaps there were authors who did not understand the significance of the evidence, but others seem to have ignored it deliberately. Curiously, the relative academic avoidance of this theme is not reflected in its fascination as a subject for discussion over dinner, or indeed as a lecture to nine- to eleven-year-old schoolchildren.

One of the objects of this book is to demonstrate the variety and distribution of toilet facilities in a large Roman town available to the 'ordinary' people. Toilets were present not only in domestic areas but also in bars and shops. There is nowhere better to see these than in the city of

Pompeii, which offers a unique opportunity to understand what facilities were available, not just to the rich and powerful but also to the ordinary working people. In the ordinary domestic buildings in Pompeii most of the toilets are for one person, but there are some houses where there may have been two or, occasionally, three seats (see Chapter 4).

Many questions arise when one looks at a Roman toilet. Did the Romans feel the same about pollution and act in the same way as we do? Did they wash their hands? We know that cultural attitudes to dirt and smell differ from place to place and from time to time. Were there social class behaviour differences relating to these questions? What were their attitudes to privacy? Did gender affect the usage of toilets?

Do toilets and waste disposal go together? A question commonly asked in modern archaeology is what did the Romans do with their waste and rubbish? Was waste discarded in the latrines? To attempt to clarify these matters, aspects of Roman drainage systems need to be investigated. Most importantly one must ask 'Did the Romans have uses for faeces and urine?' Water drainage systems have been found under streets of many Roman towns, but sewage disposal was not always integrated within the system, as will be demonstrated in Pompeii.

Having seen a small selection of toilets in the Roman world we should ask if this picture was duplicated in Britain. There were of course buildings for the Roman army and later towns and villas, and to these we shall now turn.

2

Roman Britain

Toilets for the army

Roman armies initially battled against other Italian states. Then, as the Romans expanded their territorial ambitions, the field of action spread throughout the Mediterranean and into northern Europe. Throughout the whole of the Roman Empire, and particularly on the frontiers, there is good evidence of the camps set up by Roman armies. Latrines in marching camps must of necessity have been basic – no more than trenches – and would have been backfilled on departure (see Deuteronomy 23:12-13 for disposal of human camp excrement). Little evidence of them is provided by archaeological excavation. Roman writers do not help much. Polybius, writing in the second century BCE, gives a good account of how a camp is set up, starting with the positioning of the general's tent (Polybius VI.27). From the standard placed there all the streets and the sites for the tents of the various other constituents of the legion were marked out. Unfortunately he does not mention where the latrines were to be situated. In more permanent situations the commanders of the Roman army had sufficient understanding of the requirements of their men to provide latrines for them in, or adjacent to, their forts. Initially consideration would be given to the period of time the troops were likely to remain in any particular location. Camps, which eventually became fortlets, forts or fortresses, would require different planning.

By studying Roman military establishments in Britain we may be able to answer a number of questions. Simple information should be available about the construction of the buildings and the drainage, but there are more complex issues to be addressed. What decided the size of a latrine? Is that size an indicator of the size of the garrison? Did the senior officers use it or did they have an alternative? Was any attention paid to the cultural backgrounds of the soldiers, who may have travelled up to 2000 miles from their native lands? Despite the fact that there appears to be good documentation of some of the structures within Roman forts, surprisingly little analysis has been carried out on the toilet buildings and in many of the excavation reports there is no mention of latrines. Is this the result of poor archaeology or does it imply the absence of latrines? Were there, in fact, alternatives for the disposal of human waste?

Communal latrines are the most common and vivid representation of soldiers' toilet facilities. The best preserved examples are at Housesteads

44. Garrison latrine, Housesteads fort, Hadrian's Wall.

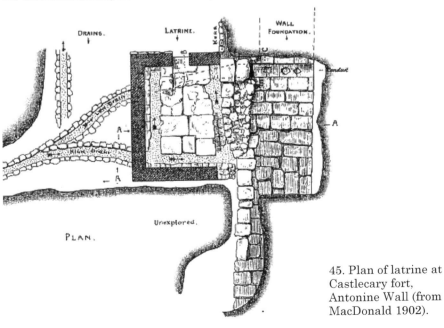

45. Plan of latrine at Castlecary fort, Antonine Wall (from MacDonald 1902).

(Fig. 44), Caerleon, Castlecary, South Shields, Vindolanda and Bearsden (Goldwater 2002: 20). These latrines are very similar in construction, but some different designs occur, notably at Piercebridge where the latrine is semicircular.

The plan of the latrine at Castlecary (Fig. 45) illustrates well the doorway into the room, the tiled floor and the complex drains which show evidence of later modifications.

On a sloping site, the latrine would often be situated at the lower end of the camp. This is exemplified by the fortlet at Barburgh Mill (Breeze 1971). Similarly the fort latrine at South Shields (Arbeia) lies against the rampart near the south-east corner (see R.J.A. Wilson 2002: 450) (Fig. 46). At Neath and Vindolanda the corner turret sites are used to house the toilets and a small latrine exists at Ebchester behind the north-west corner turret.

In later Roman army forts, elaborate drains were constructed to dispose of surface water, for the removal of waste from cavalry stable blocks and, in addition, to take human sewage out of and away from the fort. Drains in Roman forts appear to be of two types, open and closed. The open ones carry water (and possibly other materials) down through the fort. The drains, which are capped and are usually substantial, often feed into and through the latrines and then pass through the walls to allow for drainage outside the fort. This is certainly the case for the garrison latrine at Housesteads fort on Hadrian's Wall where, on a sloping site, water drains from the upper areas into a cistern, from which it is fed into the latrine to flush out the waste. The ordinary legionaries would be used to these latrines, even to the extent of emptying them. A duty roster from an Egyptian legion for 2 October 87 CE shows that a soldier, M. Longinus A[…] was on latrine duties (*ad stercus*) (P. Gen. lat. 1 verso = *CLA* 7, v; see Watson 1983: Appendix B 225).

A few forts had hospital blocks, and in some of these there is a latrine. The one at Housesteads (Fig. 47) has a water drain running through it from what is allegedly a water treatment room. The Wallsend fort hospital latrine also has a drain. In this case it runs diagonally across the room (Fig. 48). In many cases these complex water systems were supplied by aqueducts, the study of which is currently minimal. Not all sewers drained away from the forts. Tanks into which the sewage drained have been found at Ribchester and Binchester, although the latrines themselves have not been explored.

Little or nothing is known about the chronological development of fort latrines, though several stages of construction and modification have been identified for the one at Housesteads (Simpson 1976: 133-43) and many other Roman military establishments are multi-phasic.

At Prysg Field, the site of the barracks buildings of the fortress of Caerleon, the latrine is situated at the western angle of the fort (Figs 49 & 50). It measured 9 x 5 m with a drain 0.5 m wide and 60 cm deep around

46. Latrine at Arbeia fort, South Shields.

47. Hospital latrine at Housesteads, Hadrian's Wall.

48. Hospital latrine at Segedunum (Wallsend), Hadrian's Wall.

three sides. Originally this was covered by wooden seats. The flagged floor supported a shallow gutter (Nash-Williams 1931: 133-5). There is a degree of speculation about the buildings that housed these communal latrines. Were they draughty and cold? Were they fully roofed? If so, did they have windows? An enclosed roofed building would certainly have been malodorous.

These toilets are good evidence for the existence of social segregation within the army: not only were there multiple latrines for the lower ranks but the centurions had separate latrines (e.g. at Deva, where one of the Trajanic centurion's quarters had a lead-lined latrine (Frere et al. 1977) and the commandant had a latrine in his house, as also at Housesteads and at Nanstallon (Fox et al. 1972). This placement of latrines in the *praetorium* can also be seen at South Shields, Elginhaugh, Castlecary and Vindolanda (Fig. 51), where there is also a single latrine to the rear of one of the administrative offices (Goldwater 2002) (Fig. 53). In a number of cases the latrine is associated with the bath house. At Vindolanda two separate bath houses each have their own multi-seat latrine, one of which is shown in Fig. 52.

At Bar Hill the latrine lies at the lowest part of the fort and was flushed with water from the bath house, but at Chesters (Fig. 54) it is below the fort nearer to the river (R.A.J. Wilson 2002: 481). At Cramond, as well as a latrine in the north-east of the fort there was a bath house to the north of the fort. A latrine is present in Phases II and III (Alan et al. 1974; Holmes 1977). Other latrines are within the central ranges, for example at Nanstallon and Gelligaer. At Hod Hill there was a timber building comprising a row of ten open-fronted cubicles. Not all forts went to the trouble of

37

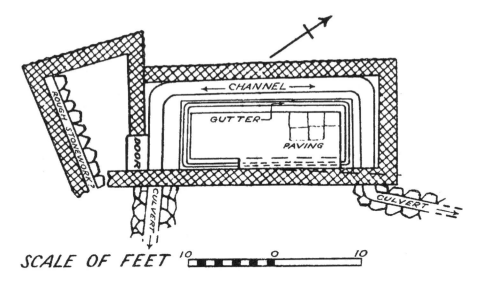

49. Plan of Prysg Field latrine, Caerleon, South Wales (from Nash-Williams 1931).

50. Latrine, Prysg Field Barracks, Caerleon.

51. Commanding officer's toilet in the *praetorium*, Vindolanda, Hadrian's Wall.

52. Ten-seat toilet in the north-east corner of the stone fort at Vindolanda.

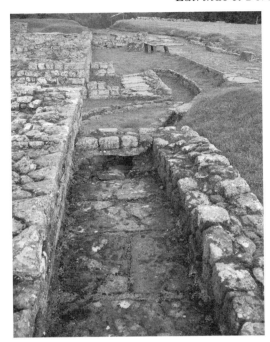

53. Single latrine in the administrative offices, Vindolanda.

54. Latrine in the bath house, Chesters Fort, Hadrian's Wall.

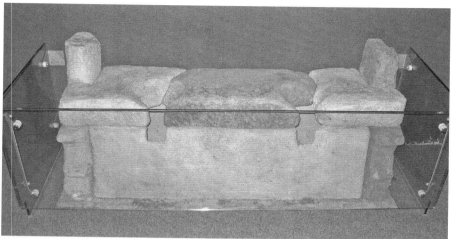

55. Reconstructed stone latrine, Segedunum Roman Fort, Baths and Museum, Wallsend.

56. Reconstructed wooden latrine, Arbeia Roman Fort and Museum, South Shields.

erecting buildings. At Valkenburg the latrines consisted of slit trenches with wooden covers, which also had removable tubs.

Only one stone seat has been found in a Roman fort in Britain. This has been reconstructed and is on display at Wallsend fort museum (Fig. 55). A reconstruction of a single wooden latrine, suggested to have been provided for the commandant, can be seen at South Shields (Fig. 56).

Did this degree of provision of toilet facilities extend to non-military sites? In order to get some indication of how much this legionary behaviour affected the habits of the general populace we need to look at the towns and villas of Roman Britain.

Toilets for civilians

It might be expected, because there are so many toilets spread throughout the Mediterranean, that the Romanisation of Britain heralded a massive change in behaviour by the Britons. If that was the case, the evidence is small. In Romano-British town houses and villas the early buildings were of wood, sometimes set onto masonry foundations. The details available from the excavation of these sites show that it is hard to be certain where the latrines were situated.

There are only a few examples of latrines in Roman towns and almost none at all in the villas, despite their numbers. There may be reasons for this deficiency. First, 'Roman' houses in Britain are few and far between, the number of towns is small and the populations within them were not large. Also they would to a large extent have been made up of indigenous people who were perhaps unaccustomed to Mediterranean cultural behaviour.

Crowding of buildings was less severe than in, for example, Pompeii, and human excrement may have been collected in buckets or chamber pots and disposed of outside the houses – either into pits or onto the land directly as manure. However, some blame for the lack of evidence could be attached to archaeologists who may have been unable, or unwilling, to identify latrines.

Two good examples of latrines in houses were at Caerwent (Venta Silurum), but unfortunately neither of these can be seen since the excavations were backfilled. The latrine in House 3 was found to be paved with large slabs of stone with a gutter which allegedly was only 'for urine on the east and south sides whilst on the west side was, as well as the gutter, a sloping channel paved with tiles over which a rail may have been fixed as a seat' (Martin & Ashby 1901). There is no evidence of a cesspit or a drain. A further example at Caerwent is House 12, now referred to as a *mansio*; this is a large building and the latrine could have seated a number of people at any one time. Fortunately the archive of the excavations, kept at Newport, has photographs of both these latrines. Another *mansio*, this time at Silchester, has a latrine adjacent to the baths.

Corbridge, just off Hadrian's Wall, has a latrine in a building south of Stanegate (R.J.A. Wilson 2002: 475). This 'town' was basically constructed to provide amenities and backup for the Roman army and culturally may reflect army behaviour rather than that of the indigenous population.

Insula XXVIII in Verulamium has two latrines, and at Wroxeter there is one, originally excavated by Bushe-Fox, which is part of a house, later modified by expansion with shops, into a sizeable block with a bath suite.

The famous villa at Chedworth has a latrine (Fig. 57). Unexpectedly, it is a good distance from the bath suite and may have been a late addition. Not all villas are as grand as Chedworth. Nevertheless we might expect

57. Latrine at Chedworth Roman villa, Gloucestershire.

that some sort of latrine would be present in these for archaeologists to pinpoint. Their apparent absence prompts us to ask how and where the inhabitants relieved themselves? Perhaps the answer is that it was easier to dispose directly of what was in fact a useful agricultural resource than to create rooms, drains and cesspits.

This dearth of information makes it difficult to draw conclusions about the use people made of these facilities. It will be much more helpful to turn to the city of Pompeii, where much more information about the development of latrines is available, if only because of the many examples found there.

3

Pompeii

Were Pompeii as near to London as it is to Naples, in a few years time not a privy would remain hid. (Engelbach 1815, quoted in Fino 2006: 112)

The events of 24 August 79 CE, so graphically described by Pliny the Younger (*Letters* VI.16 & 20), resulted in the amazing preservation of the city of Pompeii and of the bodies of its inhabitants beneath approximately 5 m of volcanic material. Nearly 1,700 years later, during the construction of an aqueduct by Domenico Fontana in 1748, discoveries were made which prompted Rocco Gioacchino de Alcubierre, who was at that time carrying out excavations in Herculaneum, to believe that the ancient city of Stabiae had been rediscovered. It was not until fifteen years later that that an inscription, discovered outside the Herculaneum Gate, allowed this buried city to be positively identified as Pompeii (Descoeudres 1994: 41). Since then, over 200 years of excavation have yielded the most comprehensive data available from any Roman imperial city. Innumerable books and articles have been written about all its different aspects, varying from studies of its paintings and mosaics to the evidence of disease in the skeletons of its inhabitants who died so tragically when Vesuvius erupted.

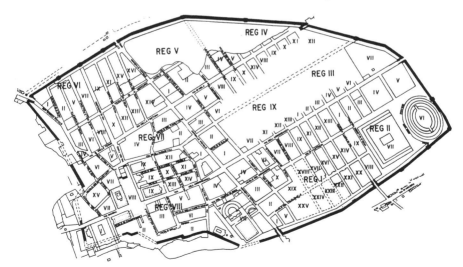

58. Plan of Pompeii showing regions and insulas.

59. Modern rubbish deposited in latrine in the House of the Priest Amandus, I.7.7.

Visitors who walk around the city can see examples of grandiose houses (with replanted gardens), workshops, bars, and of course the notorious brothel. All these relate in some way to the social structure of the people living and working in the city. However, in the guidebooks little or no attention is paid to a basic need of all these people, i.e. the toilet. This mirrors the lack of recognition by the authorities of the role played by toilets in the daily lives of the people of the city. Efforts to present the buildings to the public have ignored toilets to the extent that not only are they in poor condition but, in many cases, rubbish has been deposited in them by tourists which has been ignored by the workmen who attempt to keep the city tidy (Fig. 59). How recognisable are these facilities? Are they widespread around the city or were the inhabitants solely dependent upon public latrines? To answer these questions it is necessary to have some understanding of the system that the Romans used for the disposal of excreta. Unlike some other 'Roman' cities, Pompeii does not have an underground drainage system throughout the whole of the city. Such drains as do occur are mainly associated with the various baths (*thermae*) and were built primarily to deal with the disposal of their waste water (Fig. 60). The majority of household or domestic toilets in Pompeii drained directly into cesspits, which in general lay under the side-walks of the streets. However, some latrines were situated deep within the houses, often in the kitchen or service areas, and their cesspits were also

46

60. The drain of the
Stabian Baths.

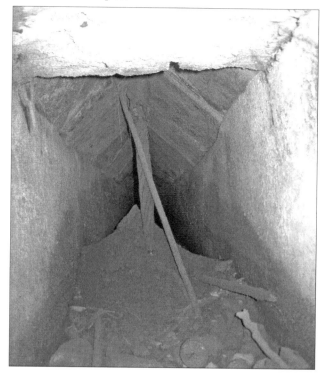

within the houses. This situation will lead us later to consider the attitudes
of the inhabitants to smell and hygiene.

The volcanic outflow spur upon which Pompeii rests is composed of
permeable rock. The cesspits can be up to 10 m deep and the human
excreta deposited into them, provided sufficient water was poured into the
cesspit, would have decayed naturally and then permeated into the subsoil. Crucial to this natural process is the question whether other
materials were deposited via the toilets into these cesspits. If so, were they
also biodegradable? Food preparation residues were deposited into the
latrine in the House of the Vestals via a terracotta pipe from the room next
door. Excavation of a large sewer in Herculaneum, which is currently in
progress, will give us more information about other types of rubbish which
were disposed of there, but there are problems with deep excavation in
Pompeii because of modern safety regulations.

The recognition of toilets in the preserved city depends upon a number
of factors. Notable in many cases are the vertical masonry pedestals upon
which rested wooden seats. The illustration of the toilet in the House of
Pansa shows this type of structure and also another feature, the tiled
surface upon which the pedestals rest and which slopes down towards the
drain in the rear wall (Fig. 61). This tiling has led modern commentators

61. Latrine in the House of Pansa, VI.6.1.

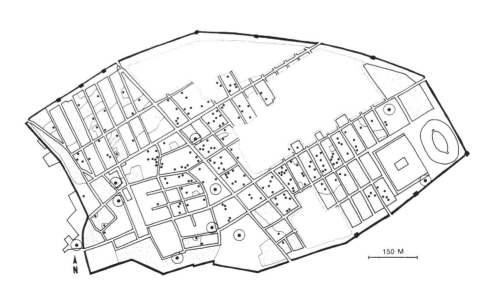

62. Distribution of latrines in Pompeii (from Jansen 2002: 59).

63. Latrine to left of entrance in VI.5.8,20.

on Roman toilets to assume that water was poured down the toilet as a cleansing agent. However there is the additional possibility that males urinated directly onto the tiles. Using these two specific diagnostic criteria, pedestals and tiling, Gemma Jansen has mapped out the distribution of toilets in Pompeii as shown in the plan (Jansen 2002: 59) (Fig. 62).

There are, however, other criteria that can be used to identify toilets. Frequently there are cuts in the walls of the rooms where the wooden seating was inserted, making masonry supports unnecessary. The latrine to the left of the entrance to VI.5.8,20 (Fig. 63) has two large pedestals with a slot in both the rear wall and north wall into which the wooden seat would have fitted. An interesting latrine occurs at IX.1.4 with two slots at right angles to each other in the kitchen area with no privacy (Fig. 64). This might suggest a triangular seat. There is a similar one at VII.15.5. Occasionally there may be one support and one slot, as seen in the illustration of VI.7.15 (Fig. 65). Sometimes there is a break in the wall plaster. The illustration of the latrine in VI.2.10 shows both the slots in the side walls for the seat and also the plastering which covers all three

49

64. Latrine in shop, IX.1.4.

65. Latrine in the House of the Duc d'Aumale, VI.7.15.

66. Latrine in VI.2.10.

67. Fragment of stone toilet seat.

walls down to the level of the seat (Fig. 66). This degree of finish of the walls suggests that these facilities were at least of a sufficient standard to be minimally comfortable, and might even have allowed for exotic decoration of the wall plaster, as in the latrine of the House of the Silver Wedding (V.7.15).

More often the evidence for the existence of the toilet is slimmer, depending upon the size of the room and its situation within the house. Even if there are no pedestals or obvious plaster demarcation lines, there may be a drain at the rear or a window in the wall separating the toilet from the street (see Fig. 78). There are, however, other criteria which can be used to identify toilets, for example stone seats. In Pompeii only one toilet with a stone seat was recorded, in IX.5.9 (Mygind 1921: 311), but unfortunately it has been lost. A chance find on a heap of masonry rubbish in a back room of IX.3.15 of a piece of stone may have been part of a toilet seat (Fig. 67). Unfortunately it is incomplete and was not found in an archaeological context.

Because there has been virtually no preservation of wood throughout the whole of the city of Pompeii, we have to rely on other evidence to recognise toilets and their positioning. The only identifying characteristics of the possible latrine in VI.2.16, 21 (Fig. 68) are the narrow room with a step up over a threshold stone and a window at the far end. From the same house an area in the kitchen with a low wall, on which a screen might have stood, and again a window, suggests the placement of a toilet (Fig. 69).

68. Latrine? in House of Narcisus, VI.2.16,21.

69. Kitchen area in House of Narcisus, VI.2.16,21.

70. Latrine with amphora in inn, I.14.2.

Only cleaning and excavation would reveal which of these places, if either or both, is the site of the facility.

Sometimes one may be surprised to see a modification of a latrine which takes a little understanding, as in the case of the latrine in I.14.2 (Fig. 70). Here an amphora has been built into the space between the pedestals. The tiled floor slopes towards a small opening at the base of the amphora. Was this done to reduce the contamination of the tiles and so that less water would be required to cleanse them?

Recent excavation has shown that movement of latrines occurred from one part of the building to another. This was part of a widespread change within the city relating to population size and social class structure which occurred in the first century CE. Typical of late change is the latrine in VII.1.36 (Figs 71 & 72). This property, a large bakery, had been expanded with an upper storey, yet the workers on the ground floor still required a latrine. In order to provide this a small room was constructed encroaching onto the property to the east (VII.1.30).

The pedestals have a foot-rest in front of them with a tiled floor into which is inserted a rectangular drain which drains the material away from the cesspit. A threshold stone has only one pivot hole and the door could not have opened outwards because the stones in the bakery are higher than the threshold. Perhaps the door folded.

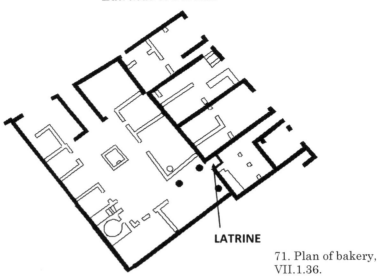

LATRINE

71. Plan of bakery,
VII.1.36.

72. Latrine in bakery,
VII.1.36.

73. Plan of large *thermopolium*, VI.8.7,8.

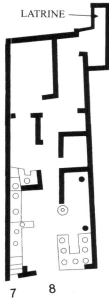

74. Latrine in large *thermopolium*, VI.8.7,8.

In order to understand the distribution of latrines throughout the city it helps to note that all types of properties may have their own toilets. It may seem obvious to assume that large houses had their own toilets. What about the lower/working classes? In the *thermopolium* (VI.8.7,8) we have a sizeable property selling food. There must have been a good choice, with fourteen *dolia* offering all manner of different foods, and there are likely to have been several people working here. Two rooms give customers places to eat or perhaps gamble, and there is a latrine at the north-east corner of the property for the use of staff and customers (Figs 73 & 74). The position of this latrine prevents its use by passers-by, which may not be the case in the next two examples.

A building somewhat larger than the the *thermopolium*, the House of Sextus Pompeius Axiochus (VI.13.12,19), has ten rooms away from the working area (Fig. 75). The latrine is immediately to the right of entrance 12. From it the access to the more élite parts of the property is along a very narrow corridor; almost certainly special visitors would not use this door

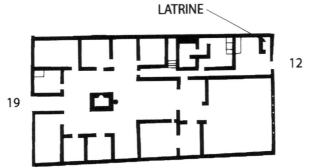

75. Plan of the House of Sextus Pompeius Antiochus, VI.13.12.

but would access the property using entrance 19. The latrine seems very convenient for the servants or slaves, and perhaps for people in the street, but was probably not used by the rich people of the house, a subject to which we will return later.

A small workshop (I.10.1), part of the insula containing the House of Menander, also has a latrine just inside the door entrance (Figs 76 & 77). Since this is so accessible from the street it is possible that passers-by may have used it without causing the people in the workshop any problems.

As is becoming obvious, the size of the property is not the governing

76. Plan of small workshop, I.10.1.

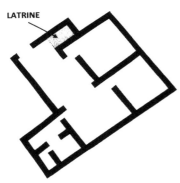

LATRINE

77. Latrine in small workshop, I.10.1.

78. Multi-seat latrine in the Forum of Pompeii.

factor as to whether it has a toilet. Latrines are not just found in bars, workshops and houses. Single-room shops line some of the main streets, especially the Via Abbondanza. Despite being very small, the shop at VIII.3.3 has its own latrine, obviously a convenience for the shopkeeper and customers.

In Roman towns one was never very far from a public toilet, although these were almost certainly exclusively male establishments. A number existed in Pompeii, an important one being in the forum. There were also multi-seat latrines in the Forum Baths, the Central Baths and the Suburban Baths.

Figs 78 and 79 show the Forum latrine and the latrine in the Suburban Baths. It has been suggested that Roman clothing may have been adequate to preserve the modesty of both sexes if these latrines were used by men and women. However, although there are a number of written references to what happened in these establishments, women are never mentioned. Where did women go when they needed a toilet? As already noted, shops and bars had toilets and it is probable that these were used by passers-by. In addition in some areas of Pompeii there are a number of single rooms opening directly from the street which have been described as latrines. Such a one, illustrated here (Fig. 80), is situated in Insula 2 of Regio VII which has a large number of shops lining its eastern and

79. Latrine in the Suburban Baths.

southern sides and would have been a busy place. The room probably had a door and would have been eminently suitable for a woman (or of course a man) caught in a moment of crisis.

Painstaking archaeological examination of all the properties in one region of Pompeii, Regio VI, has shown considerable differences in the distribution of the toilets. A property is defined as any building which is differentiable from its neighbours. Size varies, from the very large (indeed the House of the Fawn occupies one entire *insula*) to the smallest 'lock-up' shop. Not all properties have toilets, but mapping the city gives us a distribution from which we can derive a number of different inferences. The illustrations show the properties within Insulae 5 and 14 (Figs 81 & 82; downpipes are indicated by a cross in a circle).

In the eleven properties of Insula 5 there are ten toilets. Almost every property has one. Eight of the ten are in small rooms adjacent to the streets and only two are situated deep inside the house, both in kitchen areas. By contrast, in Insula 14 only four toilets can be identified and just one of these is in direct contact with the street. To a great extent this disparity

80. Toilet opening from the street at VII.2.47.

can be explained by the fact that in this *insula* there are down pipes which are evidence of six upper storey toilets serving the residential accommodation, which lies above the shops at the south of the *insula* and the bakeries and workshops at the north. Dating evidence from other parts of the city, particularly Regio VI Insula 1, suggests that this location of toilets in the upper storeys took place in the first century CE.

The excavation of a complete *insula* (VI.1) by the Anglo-American Project in Pompeii has provided a unique opportunity to study in depth the geographical, architectural and chronological distribution of latrines over a period of over 200 years, and to discuss their usage in terms of waste disposal, social class and gender, privacy, hygiene and health. It is to these data that we turn in the next chapter.

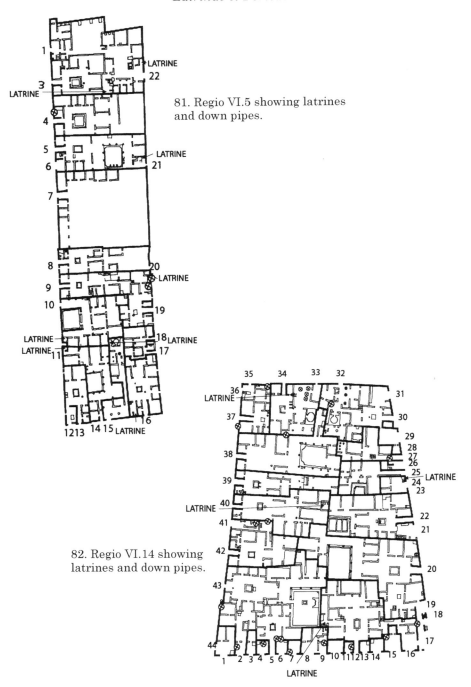

81. Regio VI.5 showing latrines and down pipes.

82. Regio VI.14 showing latrines and down pipes.

4

Chronology of toilets

Toilets existed in a number of different ancient civilisations and there is evidence of human waste disposal from houses in Mesopotamia from as early as the third millennium BCE (Wilson 2000: 153f.). At about the same time, in Mohenjo-Daro in the Indus valley there was an extensive drainage and sewerage network associated with latrines and bathrooms. Outside in the streets were some open soak-away pits. On Crete at Knossos, Sir Arthur Evans described an impressive drain which had at least one latrine emptying into it. There is also some evidence in Egypt from 18th Dynasty El Amarna, where upper-class houses have limestone seats with keyhole orifices (Wilson 2000: 158). In the Hellenic period there was considerable development of urban drainage systems, although not all cities had this refinement and the evolution of domestic latrines seems to have gone into abeyance.

The dating of latrines, which has never been considered important in itself, has always been associated with the dating of the surrounding archaeology, but the excavation of Pompeii has provided an opportunity to examine the development of domestic latrines over a period of at least 200 years and to ask and answer a number of important questions. Do we know how long toilets existed in the same place in the house? Did the construction technology change? There is, in the Roman world, an apparent difference between wooden and stone seating. Was this just a local consideration or was it a 'technical change'? Can we ascertain how long the toilets present in the 79 CE levels in Pompeii had been there, and is it known what changes, if any, had occurred since the first settlements? Were the latrines in North African Roman cities, founded after Pompeii was destroyed, any different from the ones in Italy?

Little is known of the archaeology of Pompeii prior to the year 79 CE. Indeed there have been virtually no projects designed to investigate the development and urbanisation of the city from its earliest habitation. Apart from some small excavations by Amadeo Maiuri in the mid-twentieth century, the city was left as it had been at the time of the eruption.

Over the last twenty years archaeologists have made an effort to remedy this. The work of the Anglo-American Project in Pompeii, led by Rick Jones of the University of Bradford and Damian Robinson of the University of Oxford, has concentrated on the excavation of the whole of one *insula,* Regio VI Insula 1, and excavated where possible down to natural levels. This project, uniquely, has established a diachronic picture

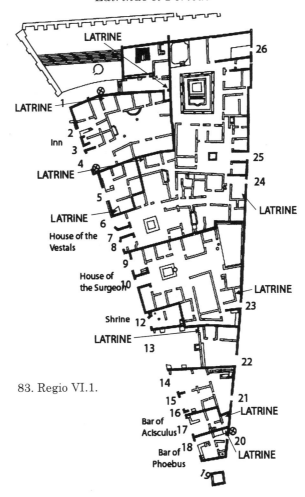

LATRINE

26

LATRINE 1

2

Inn 3

4

LATRINE

5

LATRINE 6

House of the 7
Vestals 8

9

House of
the Surgeon 10

Shrine 12

LATRINE

13

14

15

16

Bar of
Acisculus 17

Bar of 18
Phoebus

19

25

24

LATRINE

LATRINE

23

22

21

LATRINE

20

LATRINE

83. Regio VI.1.

of the evolution of a complete block of buildings at the north-west corner of the city.

Much of interest has resulted, including an understanding of the development of the toilet supply to the block, which in 79 CE consisted of two large houses, an inn with a 'restaurant', a number of bars and a religious shrine. Prior to these excavations the most obvious toilet was in the House of the Vestals (Fig. 84). This was located within the working area of what was an extremely fine house with many rooms. The cesspit was situated vertically below the seat and there was a circular masonry lid in front of the toilet allowing visual access to the pit below, and probably enabling it to be emptied.

In an earlier phase of the house there had been a toilet in a room adjacent to the rear street, the Vicolo di Narciso (Fig. 85). Towards the end

84. Latrine in the work area of the House of the Vestals, VI.1.6-8,24-26.

85. Latrine in the rear range of the House of the Vestals, VI.1.6-8,24-26.

of the first century BCE and in the early first century CE this room was a kitchen, but its use then changed and a floor was installed which closed off the toilet. This change coincided with a highly elaborate redevelopment of the house. The cesspit outside in the sidewalk of the Vicolo di Narciso remained and almost certainly had a wooden cover. The upper level of the cesspit had been raised at the time of the construction of the sidewalk. This probably happened at the same time as the paving of the road, in the late first century BCE, indicating that the toilet was still in use at that time, since otherwise it might have been filled with earth or rubbish. Excavation proceeded to a depth of about 3 m but was discontinued when it was considered unsafe to dig any deeper. Disappointingly, apart from a few iron nails, perhaps from the lid, only *lapilli* from the eruption were found in the contents of the pit. (Fig. 86).

At the same time as the toilet in the rear of the House of the Vestals was functioning there was a toilet in one of the rooms of the adjoining inn, VI.1.2. Later this was overlaid by a floor to allow the ground-floor rooms to be used as work areas and to move sleeping and residential rooms to the newly constructed upper storey to which the toilet facility was removed. As can be seen in Fig. 87, all but one of the sloping tiles had been removed so that the new floor could be laid at a reasonably low level.

86. Dr Rick Jones excavating a cesspit in the Vicolo di Narciso. Note the tile (centre left) acting as a chute from the latrine.

87. Latrine in the inn, VI.1.2.

88. Coin from cesspit in
ramp of the House of the
Triclinium, VI.1.1.

The down pipe from the upper storey which drained into the pit for this
toilet was situated in a stone buttress on the northern aspect of the wall
in VI.1.1 at the rear of the toilet. The buttress was built above the entrance
to the cesspit. The excavation of the cesspit below the buttress using
long-handled tools revealed a large amount of pottery, glassware and some
coins (Fig. 88). Fortunately this cesspit was only 2.5 m deep and could be
completely cleared. It is possible that it had been used as a rubbish
disposal pit, perhaps after the earthquake of 62 CE.

In the southern part of the *insula* a very late development in the Bar of
Acisculus, probably in the first century CE, led to the insertion of a toilet
through a *cocciopesto* floor to provide a facility for the workers and
presumably also for the customers who frequented the premises (Fig. 89).
At the time this latrine was installed there was no rear entrance to the
property from the Vicolo di Narciso (Jones & Robinson 2005), and there

89. Latrine in the Bar of Acisculus, VI.I.17.

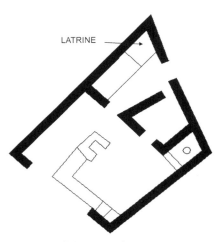

LATRINE

90. Plan of the Bar of
Phoebus, VI.1.18,20.

91. Latrine in the Bar of
Phoebus, VI.I.18,20.

92. Pipe running down
the outside of the wall
of the Bar of Phoebus in
the Vicolo di Narciso.

would have been some degree of privacy since it was in the northern corner at the rear.

In the neighbouring property to the south, the Bar of Phoebus, there was another toilet to the right of the rear doorway to the bar. The cesspit of this toilet, outside in the sidewalk of the Vicolo di Narciso, also received the contents of an upper storey latrine (Fig. 90). This time the space for the down pipe was cut into the eastern wall of the property. This was not uncommon and can be seen with many down pipes throughout the city. Fig. 91 shows a niche cut into the eastern wall, and the terracotta pipe (Fig. 92) is just visible in the upper part above the plastering. Excavation of the rest of the bar area showed that this latrine was a late addition and that there had previously been a latrine in a different part of the property which had been built over (Coppens 2006).

At one time, in an earlier phase of the building, the latrine behind the shrine (Fig. 93) was situated in a narrow room in the centre of the property. Probably in the first century CE a doorway was cut through from the shrine area, joining the properties and leaving the latrine with much less privacy than before. This aspect of Roman toilets will be discussed later.

93. The latrine behind the shrine, VI.1.22.

94. Latrine in the House of the Fisherman, VII.9.63,64.

95. The House of the Fisherman, VII.9.63,64, before and after changes.

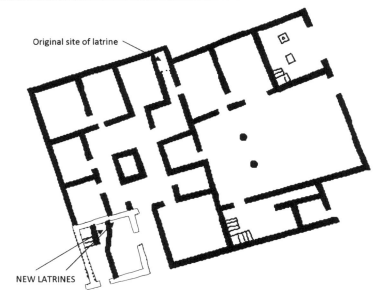

Original site of latrine

NEW LATRINES

The reasons for these changes are to some extent a matter of speculation. Certainly there appears to have been a demand for toilets within the working areas of houses and bars. The movement of living accommodation to the upper storeys, particularly if space was required for other purposes, as at the inn, suggests that social division was occurring between the rich and the less fortunate. There may also have been an increase in the population of Pompeii at around this time.

This shift of provision of toilet facilities is nowhere highlighted better than in Regio VII.9.63,64, the House of the Fisherman. Originally the latrine was at the end of a narrow corridor to the north of the house. Probably in the first century CE this latrine was sealed over and replaced by a latrine in the room immediately to the left of doorway 63 (see Figs 94 & 95). This room might then have become a work area and perhaps housed the kitchen as well as the toilet. Next door to 63 a new entrance from the street was made, giving access via a staircase to the upper storey, and to the right of the stairs another new latrine was constructed. This was now back to back with the one in 63 and emptied into the same cesspit. In addition, the staircase led to an upper storey latrine, the down pipe from which was inserted into the wall and is visible in Fig. 94 and in the Daremberg/Saglio drawing (Fig. 140). The provision here of three latrines leads one to ask who used each of them. Perhaps the one at the foot of the stairs was available to people passing by. In the south-east corner of the new latrine room in VII.9.63 there is what appears to be a rubbish disposal pit. Was the latrine cesspit not a suitable and convenient place to get rid of unwanted material? This question will be discussed in a later chapter.

There is evidence from contemporary writers that in élite houses rich owners and their families and guests used chamber pots which were emptied by slaves into the toilets in the working areas and kitchens. In the houses where the toilets were in small rooms adjacent to the outer walls this might not have applied. Here again, aspects of privacy may have prevailed – as indeed in the apparent intimate nature of toilets on the upper storeys, to which we now turn.

Upstairs toilets

Many of the buildings in Roman cities were more than one storey high. These tenements attracted comments from a number of Roman writers, including Cicero, Strabo and Tertullian. The upper storeys were used for living accommodation for the lower classes and the question arises whether or not they had toilet facilities in these 'apartments'.

In Ostia it would appear that the answer is generally in the negative, although this may be partly due to the fact that the pipes, which conveyed the effluent from the toilets above, are well covered with concrete and require a sharp eye to spot (Fig. 96). A description of the House of Diana shows that the ground floor, which was predominantly shops, also had a latrine which could have seated several people.

96. Down pipe in the barracks of the vigiles, Ostia.

97. Pipe in outer
wall, VI.6.9.

By contrast, in Pompeii the development of the upper storeys gave the inhabitants an opportunity to move the latrines upstairs. Although little now remains of the upper storeys, the down pipes, still quite obvious throughout the city, give evidence of this change. As indicated previously, it is possible that some of the down pipes in the city were just for the provision or disposal of water. In the Bar of Phoebus (VI.1.18,20) there is a cistern which was supplied by an internal pipe from the roof. This particular feature was wrongly identified as a latrine in all the references prior to the work carried out by the Anglo-American Project.

Occasionally narrow diameter (12 cm) pipes are seen which may be bringing water off a roof directly into the street. However the majority of the pipes are of wider diameter (*c.* 24 cm) and are associated with upper storey toilets. Often these pipes can be seen from the outside, usually inserted into the walls (Fig. 97) but occasionally built into buttresses.

Insertion into cuts in the walls was not the only option. Internal corners were a favourite site, with various building techniques used to enclose the

98. Internal down
pipe, VII.9.50.

pipe, as seen in VII.9.50 (Fig. 98). Most of the pipes continued downwards
inside the property. What was the reason for this? At ground level the
cesspits were usually outside in the street and it might have been easier
to run the pipes down the outside walls, although this may have restricted
the space on the sidewalks. The terracotta pipes usually slotted into each
other, fitting together tightly, but it is probable that there would have been
some odour associated with them, which may have been one of the reasons
for enclosing them.

Although other authors have commented that down pipes drain
directly onto the street, only one has been found with sufficient evidence
to justify this. Set into the outer side of the east wall of IX.1.28 is a down
pipe (Fig. 99). Here the contents of the pipe drained across the sidewalk
and caused a groove in the kerbstone. Almost certainly this carried only
water.

A great deal is known about the pottery and other ceramics of
Pompeii. Roof tiles have been found with makers' names on them. It is

99. Pipe in wall
with groove in
kerbstone, IX.1.28.

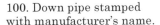

100. Down pipe stamped
with manufacturer's name.

interesting to identify at least one manufacturer of down pipes from his name
– C. Iuli(us) Nonors, stamped into the material before it was fired (Fig. 100).

Regions I, II, III, and IV do not appear to have visible latrines above the
ground floors although there are a good many down pipes in the properties
there. So far fifteen upper storey latrines have been identified in the city. In

101. Upper storey
latrine in the Shop
of Canices, V.1.30.

Regio V there are two. These occur in V.1.8 and V.1.30. Regio VI also has two, VI.15.20; VI.15.22. Regio VII has three, VII.2.18; VII.12.14; VII.12.20. There are two in Regio VIII (VIII.4.37; VIII.6.7) and six in Regio IX (IX.2.7,8; IX.2.19,21; IX.3.4; IX.3.17; IX.5.21; IX.13.1). There are also two in the arcade of shops just outside the Herculaneum gate.

   These upstairs latrines appear to be placed relatively near to where staircases have reached the upper storey, and the toilets are situated in narrow plastered niches with terracotta pipes inserted into the walls to carry the effluent down into the cesspits. The illustration of the upper storey latrine of V.1.30 (Fig. 101) shows the holes for the beams of the floor. The horizontal pedestal for the wooden seat is well defined approximately 50 cm above the floor level. The wide diameter terracotta pipes are clearly shown. What is interesting is the depth of the niche. Plans of the layout of rooms of the upper storeys do not exist, so it is impossible to judge the degree of privacy which these niches offer. Perhaps the 'family' nature of the occupants may have led to less demand for privacy.

102. Upper storey latrine in the House of C. Vibius, VII.2.18.

Not all the niches had semicircular roofing. Set into the inside of the street wall, the latrine in VII.2.18 shows the slots in the sides of the niche where the wooden seat fitted and also the tapering, easily sluiced, plaster below the seat (Fig. 102).

The property called the School House (VII.12.14) has a narrow room with two down pipes. One of these comes from the seat of the first storey latrine, while the other appears, from the scar in the wall, to be coming from a second storey latrine. This interpretation may explain a number of dual down pipes running together in walls in other parts of the city. Similarly the first storey latrine at IX.2.8 has a narrow bore pipe to the side of the niche which feeds into the main down pipe (Fig. 103). This probably carried water but just possibly may be from a second storey latrine.

It was considered possible, even with the passage of nearly 2,000 years, that mineralised faecal material might still be present within the cavities of these pipes. Scrapings were taken from a number and research at the

latrine niche

pipe from second
storey latrine?

103. First storey latrine in the House of the Loving Fountain, IX.2.8.

University of Bradford has investigated this material. Eggs of intestinal parasites, *Trichuris* and *Ascaris* species, have been discovered in nine out of ten samples of mineralised material from different down pipes, proving that faeces did indeed pass down through them (Love 2007).

6

Privacy

What is known about privacy in the Roman world? Seneca tells us that a German gladiator who suffocated himself with a sponge was allowed to go to the toilet unescorted (see p. 138). Was this out of respect for his privacy? Certainly in the public toilets associated with the bath houses there was little personal privacy. In fact there was positive fraternisation.

> *In omnibus Vacerra quod conclavibus*
> *consumit horas et die toto sedet,*
> *cenaturit Vacerra, non cacaturit.*

Vacerra spends hours in all the privies, sitting all day long. Vacerra doesn't want a shit, he wants a dinner. (Martial XI.77, tr. Shackleton Bailey)

In a second epigram Martial comments that he is now being avoided by Dento who used to seek him in the baths, theatres and toilets in order to be invited to dine.

> *Quid factum est, rogo, quid repente factum,*
> *ad cenam mihi, Dento, quod vocanti –*
> *quis credit? – quater ausus es negare?*
> *Sed nec respicis et fugis sequentem,*
> *quem thermis modo quaerere et theatris*
> *et conclavibus omnibus solebas.*
> *Sic est, captus es unctiore mensa*
> *et maior rapuit canem culina.*
> *Iam te, sed cito, cognitum et relictum*
> *cum fastidierit popina dives,*
> *antiquae venies ad ossa cenae.*

What's happened, look you, what's happened all of a sudden, Dento, that you have, four times (who would believe it?) dared to refuse my invitation? Why, you don't as much as look my way, you run away from me when I follow you – me, whom not long ago you used to seek in all the baths and theatres and lavatories? This is how it is: you're captured by a richer cuisine and the bigger kitchen has carried off the dog. Anon, and it will be soon, when the wealthy cook-shop is fed up with you, found out, and abandoned, you will come back to the bones of the old dinner. (Martial V.44, tr. Shackleton Bailey)

One of Martial's friends, Ligurinus, is a poet. However, as Martial says, you can have too much of a good thing.

> *Et stanti leges, et legis sedenti,*
> *currenti legis et legis cacanti.*

> You read to me as I stand, you read to me as I sit,
> You read to me as I run, you read to me as I shit.
> Martial III.44, tr. Shackleton Bailey

It is likely that Martial is referring here to discourse between men in public latrines. Although discourse occurred in these public places, there appears to be provision for some degree of privacy since in a number of cases a vestibule, as at the Smaller Baths of Ephesus and the Forum latrine in Pompeii, shielded the occupants from passers by. Even if there was not a vestibule, doors were commonplace, possibly including rotating doors for the Forum latrine in Ostia. Did women use these public toilets at the same time as the men? If they didn't, then where did they relieve themselves? The writers give us no help here. However, as noted earlier in Pompeii, as well as toilets in 'domestic' situations it is possible to identify a number of small narrow rooms opening directly from the street in which there are single-seat toilets (see Fig. 80).

The concept of privacy is highly complex, including physical, psychological and philosophical aspects (Kira 1970: 270). People from different cultures inhabit different sensory worlds. They not only structure space differently but experience it differently because the *sensorium*, or sensory centre of the brain, is differently 'programmed' (Hall 1968: 84). There is a selective screening, or filtering, that admits some types of data while rejecting others. Thus it is only by attempting to understand Roman culture and the behaviour it produces that we will be able to interpret the archaeological findings in terms of social stratification and change. This particularly applies to attempting to understand what privacy meant in the Roman world.

A number of latrines in private houses could have accommodated more than one person. Jansen identifies 38 such in her overview of latrines, using a width of 50 cm as a measurement for one place (Jansen 2002) – i.e. a width of less than 1 m was a single-seater (Jansen 1997: 126 n. 11). This measurement system is somewhat speculative and she modifies it in a later article (Jansen 2003: 148 n. 12). The latrine in the House of the Vestals, mentioned previously, is wide enough for two persons, using her criteria, but the internal sloping dimensions of the latrine make it more likely that it is a single-seater. Of the latrines in the remaining *insulae* of Regio VI only three are just over 1 m wide (VI.9.6,9; VI.12.1,2; VI.16.7,38). All are in large houses, but there are comparable sized properties with only single-seat latrines. Latrines with more than one seat would allow 'private'

104. Toilet in the House of the Faun, VI.12.2.

socialisation but it might be argued that there was a movement, over time, to isolate the latrine within the building and to make it, increasingly, a single-seater.

It has been suggested that 'toilets with two or more seats were most common in big workshops or in large houses where there were extensive staff' (Jansen 1997: 126), perhaps as may have been the case in the House of the Faun (VI.12.2) (Fig. 104), and indeed in the House of the Centenary, judging by the graffiti on the wall (see p. 144).

It is difficult to assess whether there were gender taboos about using the toilet within a Roman household. Certainly during the pre-imperial phase there was mixed bathing with, presumably, considerable toleration of nudity (see Nielsen 1990: 135 and n. 8). At this time the latrines associated with bath houses may even have been used by both sexes simultaneously, but it would appear that by the imperial period the socialisation that occurred within these establishments was undoubtedly masculine in nature. In Herculaneum there is a multi-seat latrine attached to the men's bath house but no such building adjacent to the women's. There is a large room to the left of the entrance which may have been used by women, but there are no toilets and other disposal methods would have had to be used, such as chamber pots.

The positioning of latrines in the parts of the large houses which might be designated working areas may have precluded the élites of both genders from using the toilets, leading them to resort instead to the use of chamber pots emptied by servants. Social and financial elevation in the first century CE, as seen in the massive reorganisation in the House of the Vestals, was not unusual. In this house the development appears to have isolated the latrine from the more opulent rooms of the house, especially the peristyle area. If there was a preponderance of male slaves within an élite household (see Harris 1999: 63) then any gender problem may have been minimal, and could have been offset by females using receptacles. Perhaps all slaves were 'invisible', even to themselves. This is likely to have been somewhat different from the busy business world of the bars on the Via Consolare, where there was a high demand for latrine facilities, perhaps primarily for male customers, though the degree of privacy offered would not preclude female usage. The late addition of a toilet in the Bar of Acisculus suggests a response to a demand.

In the *pistrinum* in Herculaneum there are two latrines serving the same workshop and these are separated by a partition (Maiuri 1954: 56). It would have been simpler to have created a two-seater. It is unlikely, but might this be an early example of separate gender toilets?

The degree of isolation within the building will undoubtedly have depended upon what options there were for the placement of the latrine (including its cesspit system), and a variety of situations has been identified, for example at the ends of corridors, under staircases, etc. (Jansen 1997: 128).

Factors for privacy may have been taken into consideration. Three such concepts have been described: 'Seen but not heard', 'Heard but not seen', and 'Not seen or heard' (Kira 1970). The degree of tolerance of these would influence, to a great extent, the ideal positioning of the latrine within the building. In a somewhat esoteric work on social interaction in the Roman houses of Pompeii, architectural boundaries are used to interpret knowledge of self through avoidance of an encounter. By creating zones of exclusion, the author states, 'architecture encloses the body and so enables aspects of the body to be kept concealed. Privacy, from this point of view, is primarily about escape from the scrutiny of others' (Grahame 2000).

When it comes to domestic toilets, as has been indicated in the previous two chapters, there appears to have been a considerable probability that the small rooms would have offered a great deal of privacy, especially if they had had doors or partitions. As a result of the lack of preservation of wood in Pompeii, no doors have been found. However, a large percentage of latrine rooms have threshold stones which have grooves into which door posts were set (Fig. 105). In the description of the latrines in the House of Menander it is stated that the latrine in I.10.7 is 'screened, on the south, by a low masonry wall and on the east, apparently, by a timber or timber-framed partition, the evidence for which is an iron-lined post hole in the floor. In fact it is likely that this is the swivel post for a wooden door and the jamb against the wall' (Ling 1997).

105. Threshold stone showing grooves for doorposts, House of the Flowers, VI.5.9.19.

The small rooms housing the toilets had varying heights of walls, frequently going right up to the ceiling. Alternatively, in some cases it would appear that there were wooden partitions on top of low walls, as preserved in Herculaneum in the Taberna Visaria. These partitions have often left wall scars indicating their presence. Many of the rooms have a step up from the floor of the corridor or outer room. This not only serves to differentiate the cubicle from other rooms, but also allows for the tile system to drain efficiently under the toilet seat.

The latrine in the Villa Sileen near Leptis Magna has a threshold stone which also has cut marks for door posts (Fig. 106). Although it is likely that this latrine is particularly associated with the bath house, there being an access door next to the latrine, it is also directly accessible to the large service areas where the servants/slaves would have been working.

Finally, as already noted, the types of clothing worn by the various classes and genders must be taken into account. It is likely that tunics and togas would have offered a considerable degree of modesty even in the presence of other people.

It seems obvious that these latrines must have been unpleasant places to visit, and shortly we must turn to considerations of Roman attitudes to the malodorous conditions that must have prevailed. However, attempts were made to decorate some latrines. This decoration in the rooms, both

slot for
door post

106. Latrine at the Villa Sileen, near Leptis Magna.

large and small, which housed the toilets, must have contributed to some degree of comfort and may have reflected other cultural influences of the times. Many of the floors were of stone flags, but decorative mosaics formed the floors of many of the later large Roman latrines throughout the Empire. This embellishment indicates that the rooms were considered sufficiently important to spend money on them. Topics illustrated range from simple designs to complex pictures. The examples from two latrines at Ostia show this variety. The latrine of the Baths of Neptune in Ostia (II.iv.2) contains a wall with some plants painted on it and a floor mosaic with a boat, a crocodile and a human figure, while there is a very simple mosaic floor, of plain tesserae, in another latrine shown in Fig. 107.

The house latrine at Bulla Regia has a mosaic floor of simple design, as do the latrines at the Villa Sileen (Fig. 106) and the villa at Sabratha (Fig. 108). Compared with these the mosaic of the 'private' latrine at the Villa del Casale in Sicily is extraordinary, with beautiful animals and birds set into a neutral background (Fig. 109). However, domestic latrines at Pompeii which predate all these mainly have simple sloping tiled floors.

Almost all the information about the rooms in which the toilets were placed comes from buildings which no longer have walls of any height; it is therefore hard to make generalisations about the decoration of toilet walls. The latrine at the Via Garibaldi in Rome has painted plaster on the

107. Simple mosaic floored
latrine, Ostia.

108. Latrine in the villa to the
south-west of Sabratha, Libya.

109. Mosaic floor of the 'private' latrine, Villa del Casale, Sicily.

back wall (Fig. 3). In Pompeii and Herculaneum many of the latrines have plaster surviving on the walls, although in the majority the colour has faded. In those where the colour survives there are only a few with decorative motifs. Fifteen of these have been described (Jansen 1993), one being the latrine in the House of Castor and Pollux (VI.9.6) (Fig. 110). This latrine, which probably seated two or three persons, has a high decorated dado, painted red. It contains yellow panel lines but no motifs. In the area above the dado a garland of flowers is visible. Its floor is mixture of herring bone and oval tiling. Occasionally, although only a small amount of wall plaster remains, the colours are striking. This can be seen in the House of Jason (IX.5.18), where the lower orange is separated from the upper red by dark red lines. VII.15.5 (Fig. 111) has decorated plaster above the seat which is inserted into adjacent wall slots, as noted previously in IX.1.4. In this case the white painted plaster would have given some lightness to the small 'room'.

Art historians have described various styles of wall painting in Pompeii and Herculaneum and attempted to assign dates to them. The information from the decoration of latrines is inadequate to give any chronology and we must look at other archaeological methods to give us some ideas about dating latrines.

First, however, we must consider the disposal of the material in the cesspit and other forms of rubbish.

86

110. Latrine in the House of
Castor and Pollux, VI.9.6.

111. Latrine in VII.15.5.

Rubbish and its disposal

Urban populations are typified by concentrations of the by-products of human activity, including excreta and discarded rubbish. The larger the city, the more waste can be generated, depending upon population size, affluence and the material conditions of urban life (Herbert & Thomas 1997). Modern Western societies have major problems with waste and it is important to reflect upon the ways in which the Romans and, in particular, the inhabitants of Pompeii, dealt with this problem.

I have already raised the question what else, other than excreta, may have been deposited in the toilets of Pompeii. Could it have been rubbish? If so, how does an archaeologist define rubbish? In using words like garbage, refuse, rubbish, and so on the implication is that this material has no significance for the living community other than as a potential problem. However, this is quite obviously an over-simplification: one person's rubbish may be part of another's livelihood. It may have cultural specificity but will reflect the individual's response within that broad base and may involve social or gender distinctions (Rathje & Murphy 1992, 133-4: Kwawe 1995). Certain types of refuse have been linked to highly charged notions of dirt and pollution (Hill 1996).

Within this particular category excrement may lie. However, nothing is ever simple; 'cow dung for example is very often considered to be a cleansing material rather than a variety of dirt' (Leach 1971: 38). Behaviours regarding the treatment of refuse relate to three characteristics of the material: the effort required to collect it and dump it, its potential re-use value, and the nuisance it offers if left where it is (Hayden & Cannon 1983). It has been suggested that there are four ways of dealing with rubbish: dumping, burning, recycling and minimising the volume of material which produces rubbish (Rathje & Murphy 1992: 33). From a practical point of view these are the ways in which the Romans dealt with their rubbish.

These are not the only methods of classification. Another discussion of the concepts of pollution and taboo considers that 'dirt' exists in the eye of the beholder. It offends against order and, in particular, has great significance within religious doctrines (Douglas 1966).

Archaeologists tend to define a deposit as rubbish if it has some or all of the following characteristics: 'If it occurs outside, versus inside buildings, if many different materials are mixed together, if there is a high density of material (pottery sherds, bones, charcoal, glass), if the finds tend to be broken or if they are ashy, but not *in situ*. ... Implicit in this is an assumed distinction between clean and unclean, pure and impure, useful and not-useful, desirable and undesirable' (Martin & Russell 2000: 59). These different typologies have been designed to fit the varying patterns they describe. None appears to cover all eventualities, and it is necessary to adopt a more flexible approach, incorporating a number of these issues into the discussion.

Archaeologically refuse can be defined as primary or secondary. Primary deposits are those found in association with specific activities carried out in the area of excavation, e.g. cooking areas. The kitchen in a small house in Pompeii (VI.2.27) has a cooking surface and a niche latrine in the same small room. Between them is a circular cover set into a square stone slab (Fig. 112). This could be raised by pulling on a metal ring, giving access to the cesspit. Would kitchen waste have been deposited here? That seems unlikely as the latrine is only a matter of a metre away and would have been very convenient for refuse disposal.

Analysis of archaeological bone debris shows that smaller and finer debris (the remains of small and medium sized animals that were less subject to butchery) is more likely to be visible close to where it was dropped, in or near to domestic activity areas. Conversely, the bones from larger animals are more likely to be deposited elsewhere as a result of post-butchery practices (Wilson 1989).

A slightly different understanding is that 'most animal bone is discarded at one of three stages – after slaughter and butchery, after the preparation of food, or after eating' (Halstead et al. 1978). For a wider discussion of the nature of archaeological bone samples from rubbish see Hesse and Wapnish 1985: 18-32.

There is a type of Roman mosaic known as *asaroton* ('unswept') that depicts a floor covered in discarded food material from banqueting. If this is indicative of the cultural behaviour of privileged Romans dining in their solid-floored dining areas, it seems most likely that the waste was cleaned away afterwards. Was it deposited in the latrine or were pits dug for the disposal of such material?

The excavation of *insula* VI.1 at Pompeii has resulted in the accumulation of data covering a period of approximately 400 years. It is highly likely that, over such a lengthy period of time, there was an element of change in rubbish disposal. For example, there are five distinct levels of deposition on a rubbish dump by a wall at Qasr Ibrim, Egypt, which had accumulated over a period exceeding two centuries (Adams 1985). Analysis of levelling deposits or materials used when floors were raised in Pompeii may help to define what constituted rubbish from one period to another, and as an additional benefit may give indications of social class.

The original excavation of VI.1 took place in the late eighteenth century. Since then it has been subjected to 200 years of wear and tear as well as serious damage inflicted by Allied bombing in 1943. As a result there has

112. Latrine in VI.2.27, showing niche and 'inspection cover'.

been little obvious evidence of rubbish in the accessible parts of the properties. Two areas suggestive of primary rubbish deposits were excavated in 1996. In the small area between two walls to the south-west of the peristyle of the House of the Vestals a large deposit was discovered containing 600 pieces of ceramic including 100 sherds of late *terra sigillata* as well as bath flue tiles. Other finds included painted plaster, animal bone (twenty items) and a dozen nails with a few single items such as an ivory ring, a single bronze coin and an unidentifiable copper alloy artefact. It is likely that all these had remained *in situ* for nearly 2,000 years, even allowing for the original excavation in the late eighteenth century. Similarly in another area a large deposit of material was excavated which included painted plaster, animal bone, more than 30 metal artefacts (both iron and copper alloy), some pieces of shell (10), a gaming piece, some glass, a lead sling shot and a loom weight. This deposit was situated in an isolated part of the House of the Vestals under the staircase leading to the upper storey from the kitchen area. The relative seclusion of these deposits suggests that there was no urgency in their removal, and perhaps that they had some value, or that it was too much trouble to remove the material.

Small amounts of domestic waste have been found in a number of situations in VI.1, especially in drains (Ciaraldi & Richardson 1999). This has provided information, particularly about diet, but is no real indicator of rubbish disposal except to say that perhaps it would eventually have been washed into the street. In the House of Amarantus (I.9,11-12) piles of amphorae were found in different areas, having been buried *in situ* by the 79 CE eruption Some of these were piled tidily, upside down, suggesting that they might be for re-use. Others were in a pile along with a damaged sundial and a heavily sooted pan with a broken handle. This might suggest some degree of disorder, but the items may only have been waiting to be resorted prior to re-use/disposal. A third group of amphorae were more casually disposed, different in range and included a broken bowl of Italian *sigillata* (Berry 1997a, 1997b).

These separate piles may reflect some attitudes to tidiness within the house. They may also reflect a degree of disorder following the major earthquake which hit the Bay of Naples area in 62 CE.

The disposal of material seen as either 'clean' or 'dirty' rubbish is influenced by the status of the disposer and often, to various degrees, associated with the religious or secular beliefs of any particular society. Is it conceivable that the position of rubbish within the space of the property indicates the social position of people living or working in those areas?

Rubbish would also have accumulated in the streets. In the excavation of the Vicolo di Narciso a large deposit of ceramics and amphorae was found on the sidewalk against a wall opposite the House of the Vestals (Hobson 1998; AAPP Excavation AA110). There was considerable damage to this material, which may have been waiting to be collected and re-used. In Rome, responsibility for the cleaning and maintenance of the street outside a house rested with the owner or occupier of the property. If he failed to do this the aediles would have the job done by contractors and charge the cost to the negligent owner (Liebeschuetz 2000: 55).

It has been suggested that wine and fish-product amphorae were washable and hence 're-cyclable' but that oil amphorae were less amenable to cleaning and more likely to be discarded (or re-used as building or flooring materials) (Rodriguez-Almeida 2002). The question has been raised: 'Were there collections of rubbish from a number of source sites with selection or exclusion of particular categories of rubbish and transport to a central dump?' (Wilson 2002). Hordes of garbage pickers in Mexico City have been described systematically searching through the heaps of rubbish delivered to the city's dumps. Similarly, in Cairo, the 'scavenging *zabaline* manage to recycle 80% of what they pick up' (Rathje & Murphy 1992: 193). Would impoverished inhabitants of Pompeii have behaved in a similar manner?

A black glaze pottery kiln dump was found near the Basilica in Pompeii (Arthur 1986: 40). Was this waiting to be removed, or could some of the material have been recycled in the manufacturing process? Wandering through dark streets in the middle of the night, the heroes of the *Satyricon* cut their feet on jagged stones and 'jutting fragments of broken jars' (Petronius *Satyricon* 79). In this case, rather than being recycled, it appears that the pottery was either just rubbish thrown out into the road or had been deliberately put there to be trodden in to improve the surface. The latter would not be the case in the later phases of Pompeii, when the majority of the roads had been surfaced with stone.

Particularly during the first century CE, following the introduction of piped water from the aqueduct, water from house fountains exited via drains under door thresholds onto the street. This, together with rain-water and perhaps the overflow from street fountains, would have contributed to the removal of surface rubbish from the streets. Pompeii was fortunate in that the sloping nature of the terrain allowed the street drainage system to drain out the rainwater as fast as possible.

As mentioned earlier, small amounts of rubbish have been found deposited within the drains leading out of the properties into the streets (Ciaraldi and Richardson 1999). These drains were not intended primarily for the disposal of rubbish, but to channel water from *impluvia* and fountains. That fraction of the material which was washed through would have contributed to the larger quantities of refuse lying in the streets derived from other sources, such as animal droppings. Also the street-side bars provided food, some of which would have been eaten on the street and may have produced discarded waste. Only by sectional excavation of one of the narrow unpaved side streets might some evidence of rubbish accumulation be found.

In some houses a tiled surface may not necessarily signify a toilet. In the corner of one of the houses in the southern part of Pompeii (I.17.3) is a quarter of a circle feature with a drain leading out – presumably into a cesspit (Fig. 113). There is no evidence that this is a toilet and one might assume that it is for rubbish disposal, possibly of a 'watery' nature. Similar chutes occur elsewhere, one being at floor level alongside the kitchen working surface in VIII.2.24 (Fig. 114). This type of liquid rubbish disposal gutter was called a *trua* (Scobie 1986: 410 n. 88).

A feature found in VIII.4.53 might also be for rubbish disposal. This is a large diameter pipe set into the corner of the wall (Fig. 115). It does not appear to be descending from above and might repay excavation to clarify its purpose.

In Rome, and presumably in other cities during the early imperial period, the aediles were responsible for keeping the streets clean. Julius Caesar's law of 44 BCE on municipalities states that each owner of property fronting on the streets of Rome is responsible for keeping his part of the street in good repair, and should also ensure that no water stands there

113. Rubbish disposal feature (?) in inn, I.17.3.

114. Waste chute (?), in VIII.2.24.

115. Rubbish disposal feature (?) in workshop, VIII.4.53.

prohibiting public passage (*CIL* I.206 *Tabula Heraclensis, vulgo lex Iulia municipalis*; see Abbott & Johnson 1926: 288-98: Panciera 2000: 99). The law explicitly states that in no way should this obligation prevent the aediles or quattuorvirs from cleaning the streets (Johnson et al. 1961: 94). Suetonius comments that when Vespasian was aedile, he apparently failed in this duty:

> *Mox, cum aedilem eum Caius Caesar, succensens curam verrendis viis non adhibitam, luto inssisset oppleri congesto per milites in praetextae sinum*
> ...

> Then, when he (Vespasian) was aedile, Caius Caesar, incensed at his neglect of his duties of cleaning the streets, ordered that he be covered with mud, which the soldiers accordingly heaped into the bosom of his purple-bordered toga. (Suetonius *Vespasian* V.3, tr. Rolfe)

There was dirt in the streets then, just as there can be today. As Juvenal comments, *pinguia crura luto* ('my legs are besplattered with mud', *Satire* III.248, tr. Ramsay). Walking around at night might involve a number of hazards, among them the contents of chamber pots, or even the pots themselves:

Respice nunc alia ac diversa pericula noctis:
quod spatium tectis sublimibus unde cerebrum
testa ferit, quotiens rimosa et curta fenestris
vasa cadant, quanto percussum pondere signent
et laedant silicem. Possis ignavus haberi
et subiti casus inprovidus, ad cenam si
intestatus eas: adeo tot fata, quot illa
nocte patent vigiles te praetereunte fenestrae.
Ergo optes votumque feras miserabile tecum,
ut sint contentae patulas defundere pelves.

And now regard the different and diverse perils of the night. See what a
height it is to that towering roof from which a potsherd comes crack upon
my head every time that some broken or leaky vessel is pitched out of the
window! See with what a smash it strikes and dents the pavement!
There's death in every open window as you pass along at night. You may
well be deemed a fool, improvident of sudden accident if you go out to
dinner without having made your will. You can but hope, and put up a
piteous prayer in your heart that they may be content to pour down on you
only the contents of their slop-basins (Juvenal *Satires* III.268-77, tr.
Ramsay)

In some houses the cesspits were only deep enough to house a large
amphora or a *dolium*. When full, these receptacles would probably be
removed by *stercorarii* and replaced by another vessel. It is unlikely,
though not impossible, that the contents of one of these could have been
thrown out over a balcony. City administrators were told not to allow
anyone to fight in the street, or to fling dung, or to throw out any dead
animals or skins. In a letter discussed in the collection of legal documents
entitled *Fontes Iuris Romani Antejustiniani* (*FIRA*), an interesting legal
situation arises in which a house is being 'besieged' by angry neighbours.
The owner of the house instructs a slave to drive away the yobs by
throwing excrement onto them. The servant, either on purpose or inadver-
tently, throws the container as well as its contents, resulting in the death
of one of the besiegers (*FIRA* III.185). We do not know the upshot of this
particular event, but if a falling object caused the death of a freeman a fine
of fifty *aurei* was levied and if physical injury short of death occurred then
the loss of wages, medical fees and other expenses incurred had to be
reimbursed (*Digest* 43.10.1.3-5 Papinian).

Wherever rubbish is deposited it may undergo processes of natural
decomposition. During this period it is likely to be accessed by scavengers.
A variety of these existed in ancient Egypt, including dogs, cats, rats, mice,
birds and crocodiles (Dixon 1989). All but the last are likely to have been
inhabitants of Pompeii throughout the period of its urbanisation and will
have had an effect not only on the discard behaviours of the human
population but also on the archaeological patterns we interpret. Questions
of food residue disposal may relate to household animals, especially dogs

of which we know there were a considerable number in the city, their skeletons having been found in the excavations (Richardson et al. 1997: 95-6). These may not have been the only skeletons lying about in Roman cities.

> *Quisquis stolaeve purpuraeve contemptor*
> *quos colere debet laesit impio versu,*
> *erret per urbem pontis exul et clivi,*
> *interque raucos ultimos rogatores*
> *oret caninas panis inprobi buccas;*
> *illi December longus et madens bruma*
> *clususque fornix triste frigus extendat:*
> *vocet beatos clamitetque felices,*
> *Orciviana qui feruntur in sponda.*
> *At cum supremae fila venerint horae*
> *diesque tardus, sentiat canum litem*
> *abigatque moto noxias aves panno*

Whoever he be, despiser of stole or purple that has assailed with impious verses those whom he ought to respect, let him wander through the city exiled from bridge and slope and last among hoarse beggars crave morsels of shameless bread fit only for dogs. May a long December and a wet winter and a closed archway drag out for him miserable cold. May he call them happy, acclaim them fortunate who are borne in an Orcivian litter. But when the threads of his final hour have come and his tardy day of death, let him hear the wrangling of dogs and flap his rags to drive off noxious birds. (Martial X.5, tr. Shackleton Bailey)

This dying beggar hears the howls of scavenging dogs and the wings of carrion crows. His body may well have lain in the street for some time. Suetonius narrates that while Vespasian was breakfasting a stray dog brought a human hand from a crossroads into the dining room and dropped it under the table (Suetonius *Vespasian* V.4). The only human bone found during the excavations in VI.1 was discovered in a cesspit on the ramp leading up to the House of the Triclinium, VI.1.1. There is no easy explanation for this solitary bone, but it may reflect the disposal of bodies left lying in the streets. Although much of the population belonged to extended family groups, those at the lowest end of society were so poor that their corpses could be left lying around. When the Emperor Nero was fleeing from Rome, his horse shied at the smell of a decomposing body lying by the roadside (Suetonius *Nero* 48). It has been estimated that about 1,500 corpses a year had to be removed in Rome (Bodel 2000: 129). This is reflected in the tale of a Gaul who fell in the road and could not get up. However aid was at hand:

> *Quattuor inscripti portabant vile cadaver*
> *accipit infelix qualia mille rogus;*

Four branded slaves were bearing a corpse of low degree like a thousand that the pauper's pyre receives; (Martial VIII.75.9-10, tr. Shackleton Bailey)

The slaves dump the corpse and carry the injured man home. In Rome the corpses of vagrants and the homeless were simply thrown into open pits, as in the Esquiline Field (Robinson 1992: 125). However, in the aftermath of Sejanus' downfall (33 CE) 'rotting bodies were dragged into the Tiber ... with none to cremate or touch them' (Tacitus *Annals* VI.16). Euripides comments that children were thrown into rivers, flung into dung-heaps and cess trenches, and exposed on every hill and roadside, 'a prey for birds, food for wild beasts to rend' (Euripides *Ion* 504). Notably, in the Athenian Agora a well was uncovered containing the remains of 175 babies thrown there to drown. Some abandoned children in Rome were 'rescued' and ended up as slaves with cognomens such as Stercorosus or Stercorius (*stercus* = dung, excrement).

> *Transeo suppositos et gaudia votaque saepe*
> *ad spurcos decepta lacus, saepe inde petitos*
> *pontifices*

> I say nothing of spurious children, changelings, picked up beside some filthy cistern, and passed off as richly born (Juvenal *Satires* VI.602, tr. Braund)

As well as dogs, vermin abounded and would have been attracted to rubbish both inside the houses and outside in the streets (Dixon 1972: 31f.). Can archaeology provide information concerning the degree of influence scavengers may have had in the disposal of rubbish? That such were present in Pompeii has been noted in excavations of cisterns near the Temple of Apollo. Here, along with the bones of pig and sheep, were those of Spanish and house mouse, rat and weasel (Arthur 1986: 35). The last of these is mentioned by both Pliny the Elder and Petronius, and one weasel bone was found in the 2004 season excavation of the Anglo-American Project in Pompeii (Jane Richardson, AAPP animal bone specialist).

> *Mustelarum duo genera, alterum silvestre, distant magnitudine, Graeci vocant ictidas ... Haec autem quae in domibus nostris oberrat et catulos suos, ut auctor est Cicero, cottidie transfert mutatque sedem, serpentes persequitur.*

> Of weasels there are two kinds, one wild and larger than the other, called by the Greeks *ictis* ... The other kind, however, which strays about our homes, and moves daily, as Cicero tells us, its nest and kittens, chases away snakes. (Pliny the Elder *Natural History* XXIX.16, tr. Jones)

> *Cicaro meus ... Ego illi iam tres cardiles occidi, et dixi quia mustella comedit.*

> My little boy ... I killed three of his goldfinches just lately, and said that the weasel had eaten them. (Petronius *Satyricon* 46, tr. Heseltine, revised Warmington)

7. Rubbish and its disposal

In the Middle Ages keeping large numbers of animals such as geese, ducks and hogs was a common practice, to the extent that in the fifteenth century a number of cities forbade their citizens to let their pigs roam the streets (Varron 1939: 208). This echoes Ergasilus in Plautus' play *Captivi*, who pretends to be an inspector of nuisances and declaims:

> *Tum pistores scrofipasci qui alunt furfuribus sues,*
> *quarum odore praeterire nemo pistrinum potest:*
> *eorum si quoiusquam scrofam in publico conspexero,*
> *ex ipsis dominis meis pugnis exculcabo furfures.*

> And as for the millers that keep sows and feed waste stuff to their swine that raise such a stench that nobody can go by the mill. If I spy a sow of any one of them on the public highway I'll up with my fists and stamp the stuffing out of those sows' owners (Plautus *Captivi* 807-10, tr. Nixon)

Little is known about animals roaming freely in Roman streets, but soiling by horses (and other equines) and dogs, is highly likely to have occurred. There is evidence for the existence of a rudimentary public service for the disposal of rubbish in Rome in both the republican and imperial periods (Panciera 2000).

In Pompeii, during the imperial phase of the city, it would appear that pits were dug for the disposal of rubbish. Some of these were found in front of the *tabernae* which fronted onto the Via del Foro (Arthur 1986: 38). It is possible that these pits were dug for reasons other than disposal of rubbish and that the fills are purely a convenient disposal method.

Caesar's law on municipalities states that *plostra stercoris expotandei caussa* ('carts for the purpose of carrying out dung') were permitted to enter Rome during the daytime, when most wheeled traffic was prohibited (see Abbott & Johnson 291: 66f.). The law states that 'no one shall drive a wagon along the streets of Rome after sunrise or before the tenth hour of the day except *whatever will be proper*' (113.14; my italics). It is modified in 113.16, which states that 'it is not in the interest of the city to prevent ox wagons or donkey wagons that have been driven into the city by night from going out empty, or from carrying out dung from within, after sunrise until the tenth hour' (Johnson et al. 1961: 95: also Liebeschuetz 2000: 53).

Perhaps there was little need to empty the cesspits in Pompeii, but certainly they were emptied in Herculaneum, as a graffito scratched into a column of the peristyle of the House of the Black Room (VI.11) tells us: *Exempta sic stercora a XI asibus* ('Dung from this (cesspit) was emptied for eleven *asses*', *CIL* IV.10606). Trajan, writing to Pliny the Younger about problems in his province, mentions the cleansing of public baths and sewers by long-term criminals:

> *Si qui vetustiores invenientur et senes ante annos decem damnati, dis-*
> *tribuamus illos in ea ministeria, quae non longa a poena sint. Solent enim*

eius modi ad balineum ad purgationes cloacorum, item munitiones viarum et vicorum dari.

But where more than ten years have elapsed since their conviction and they are grown old and infirm, let them be distributed in such employments as approach penal servitude; that is, either to attend upon the public baths, cleanse the common sewers, or repair the streets and highways, the usual offices to which such persons are assigned. (Pliny the Younger *Letters* X.32, tr. Radice)

There is some written evidence to suggest that carts carried away house refuse of various types, including that from latrines. In a story related by Valerius Maximus a man is dreaming of the murder of his friend who appeals to him for revenge:

Corpus enim suum a caupone trucidatum tum maxime plaustro ferri ad portam stercore coopertum.

For his body, said he (in the dream), done to death by the innkeeper, was at that moment being carried to the gate in a wagon, covered with dung. (Valerius Maximus *Memorable Doings and Sayings*, tr. Shackleton Bailey)

Messalina, fleeing from Claudius, uses an unlikely means of transport:

Atque interim, tribus omnino comitantibus – id repente solitudinis erat – spatium urbis pedibus emensa, vehiculo, quo purgamenta hortorum excipiuntur (eripiuntur) Ostiensem viam intrat.

Meanwhile, with three companions in all (so complete suddenly was her solitude), she covered the full breadth of the city on foot, then mounted a vehicle used as a receptacle for garden refuse, and took the road to Ostia. (Tacitus *Annals* XI.32, tr. Jackson)

The garden refuse alluded to above is the subject of advice from the agricultural writer Columella:

... solido vel stercore aselli,
armentive fimo saturet ieiunia terrae
ipse ferens holitor diruptos pondere qualos,
pabula nec pudeat fisso praebere novali
immundis quaecumque vomit latrina cloacis.

... the gardener should with rich mould or asses' solid dung
or other ordure, glut the starving earth,
bearing full baskets straining with the weight.
Nor should he hesitate to bring as food
for new ploughed, fallow ground whatever stuff
the privy vomits from its filthy sewers.
Columella On Agriculture X.81-5, tr. Forster & Heffner

Semi-storage in heaps of manure was not uncommon in Roman towns. In Ostia there were, it seems, many fewer toilets in private areas than in Pompeii. In a description of the *insulae* of imperial Ostia only sixteen were described (Reg. I: ii.5; iii.3,4; vi.1; vii.1; xi.2,3; xii.1; Reg. II: iv.3; v.1; Reg. III: i.9; v.1; vii.5; x.1; xii.1,2; Reg. V: ii.8; iii.3; iii.4) (Scobie 1986: 414ff., quoting Packer). Five of these were situated under staircases and there is much less evidence for upper storey latrines. The reason for this apparent deficit may be related to the high water table in Ostia, making the disposal of sewage a problem. Two large dungheaps, one next to the eastern gate, the other in the city centre, might suggest a different solution, perhaps involving wooden toilets with 'buckets'. This also might explain the large number of public latrines throughout the city from which the excreta was removed via sewers.

Analogous to the situation in Roman towns was that in the Middle Ages, when the cleansing of the streets was included in the municipal administration of a number of European cities. Citizens were implored not to put their garbage in front of their neighbour's house. Regulations in Nuremberg stated that rubbish in front of houses must be removed every four days, and in Frankfurt and Douai every eight days. In London, in 1671, the common Council enacted that no 'goung-fermer' should carry ordure till after 10.00 pm in winter and 11.00 pm in summer, and provided a penalty of 13s 4d for any of them convicted of spilling such in the streets (Sabine 1934: 317).

Roman civilisation produced a great amount of rubbish, much of which was discarded. There is, however, evidence of the recycling of certain types of materials. The recycling of discarded amphorae was mentioned above. Metal work would normally either be repairable or the metal might be of sufficient value to be re-used in a different way (Rodriguez Almeida 2002: 124). It is difficult to assess exactly how much reprocessing of metal there was. Certainly the excavation of VI.1 at Pompeii has produced two large trays full of metal, mainly iron and copper alloy. Juvenal describes the recycling of metal (note the allusion to chamber pots):

iam strident ignes, iam follibus atque caminis
ardet adoratum populo caput et crepat ingens
Seianus, deinde ex facie toto orbe secunda
fiunt urceoli pelves, sartago, matellae.

Now the flames are hissing, now that head, idolised by the people is glowing from the bellows and the furnace: huge Sejanus is crackling. Then the face that was number two in the whole world is turned into little jugs, basins, frying pans and chamber pots. (Juvenal *Satires* X.60-5, tr. Braund)

Archaeological evidence in the House of the Vestals has indicated that some of the lead piping leading to decorative fountains was removed, probably after the earthquake in 62 CE. It is not known what became of it.

There does not appear to be any evidence of stockpiling of lead pipes for re-use in Pompeii. However, it is possible that, had the early excavators in the Bourbon period found such stockpiling, they would have just removed it because it would have been a valuable commodity for them. There is little evidence in Rome for the re-use of lead piping, probably because there was only infrequently cause to disturb it (Rodriguez Almeida 2002).

Broken glass was a valuable commodity (Leon 1941) and Martial alludes to it being bartered in exchange for sulphur 'matches', used for lighting fires and lamps.

> *Urbanus tibi, Caecili, videris:*
> *non es, crede mihi. Quid ergo? Verna,*
> *hoc quod Transtiberinus ambulator*
> *qui pallentia sulphurata fractis*
> *permutat vitreis ...*

> You fancy yourself a wit, Caecilius. Believe me, you are not. What then? You are a vulgar buffoon. What you are, the cheapjack from across the Tiber is, who barters yellow sulphur matches for broken glass ... (Martial I.41, tr. Shackleton Bailey)

The people who carried on this trade (*scrutarii*) were the equivalent of rag-and-bone men. Martial is not the only writer who alludes to the barter of broken glass. In a description of an entertainment given by the Emperor for a Saturnalia, Statius describes the various groups of participants and observers:

> *hic plebs scenica quique comminutis*
> *permutant vitreis gregale sulphur*

> Here are theatre-folk and (also) those who barter common sulphur for broken glass. (Statius *Silvae* I.vi.73-4, tr. Shackleton Bailey)

Martial alludes to glass dealers a second time, in particular the collectors of broken glass beakers (*Vatinians*):

> *Vernaculorum dicta, sordidum dentem,*
> *et foeda linguae probra circulatricis,*
> *quae sulphurato nolit empta ramento*
> *Vatiniorum proxenata fractorum ...*

> ... quips of home-bred slaves, vulgar abuse, and the railings of a hawker's tongue, such as a dealer in broken Vatinians would not want to buy for a sulphur match ... (Martial X.3, tr. Shackleton Bailey)

This broken glass was certainly collected for recycling in Roman Britain (Price & Cool 1991: 23). There is a possibility that the expression *fracta vitrea* may have been used as slang for rubbish in general.

7. Rubbish and its disposal

Quid ego, homo stultissime,
facere debui cum fame morerer?
An videlicet audirem sententias,
id est vitrea fracta et somniorum interpretamenta?

What was I to do, you big fool
when I was dying of hunger?
Was I to listen to his lecturing
a lot of broken glass, and dream interpretations?

Petronius Satyricon 10, tr. Walsh

This brief summary of the factors influencing the deposition and disposal of rubbish in a Roman city demonstrates how difficult it is to draw hard and fast conclusions from the archaeology when formation processes have modified the original deposits. Perhaps looking at more of what the Romans wrote will give us better insights into their culture and behaviour – as reflected in their cultural responses to dirt and smell.

8

Dirt, smell and culture

It is impossible, when covering the subject of human excrement, not to comment upon the principles of hygiene/cleanliness which may have been operated in Roman times. Opinions vary about the degree of under-standing, during this period, of the nature of the transmission of disease. Suffice it to say that the remarkable modern emphasis upon personal and civic hygiene has only come about since the mid-nineteenth century. It would appear that in Roman times there were standards affecting pollu-tion and indecency, but these were not necessarily associated with control-ling the spread of disease.

There were some standards of personal hygiene (Scarborough 1980: 37). For example lice were dealt with by burning the clothes containing them. This may explain the humour evoked by Trimalchio (in Petronius' *Satyri-con*) drying his hands on the hair of his slave, which might have been infested with lice.

It is clear that the Greeks and Romans had no definite understanding of the concept of public health relating to urban pollution (Nutton 2000: 72). If we are inclined to believe that men urinated openly in the street, then what about women? There is some evidence that suggests that both urination and defecation in the wrong places were considered to be pollution. Juvenal is critical of two élite women, Tullia and Maura, who defiled the image of Pudicitia at the altar of chastity in the Forum Boarium in Rome.

> *Noctibus hic ponunt lecticas, micturiunt hic*
> *effigiemque deae longis siphonibus implent ...*

> It is here that they halt their litters at night and it is here that they piss and fill the goddess's image with their powerful streams ... (Juvenal *Satires* VI.309-10, tr. Ramsay)

Pudicitia was originally specific to patrician women and women who had married only once, and we need to know more about these two ladies to understand the motive behind their behaviour. Urinating on statues was not the only way of defiling them. According to the following comment by Juvenal, either urination or defecation would serve the purpose.

> *... inter quas ausus habere*
> *nescio quis titulos Aegyptius atque Arrabarches,*
> *cuius ad effigiem non tantum meiiere fas est.*

And those triumphal statues, amongst which some Egyptian Arrabarch
or other has dared to set up his titles, against whose statue more than one
kind of nuisance may be committed (Juvenal *Satires* I.131, tr. Ramsay)

A mosaic in the entrance of a house in Timgad (Thamugadi) shows a
black-skinned workman carrying a spade. His large phallus may be considered to be good luck. However, he is urinating freely (Germain 1969: pl.
XLII) (Fig. 116). This appears to be contradictory to beliefs about urination
being polluting. Is it possible that this is a joke? One researcher originally
suggested that the image might be designed to deter the evil eye (Dunbabin 1978). Later, the same author stated positively that the figure is
ejaculating and that he signifies the devil with a fire shovel, to be walked
upon as you enter the baths (Dunbabin 1989: 42).

It seems unnecessary to ask if the toilets would have smelt. Smells
travel more effectively in humid air (Bartosiewicz 2003: 179). We have
already seen that in Pompeii some of the rooms housing toilets had
windows. These would have provided not only some light but also a
degree of ventilation. However, there is evidence that there was glass
in some of the windows. Was there any other method available to
control the smell? Emptying hot charcoal from the kitchen into the

116. Mosaic from
Timgad (from Germain
1969, pl. XL11).

117. Vaulted room, House of the Banker, VI.7.20-2.

toilets would have sealed the contents and burnt off the methane produced by decomposition of the excreta. Unfortunately there is little archaeological evidence of this practice. It is unlikely that any of the rooms were roofless and open to the elements. Although most of the city has virtually no surviving upper storeys, ceilings or roofs, there are rooms containing toilets which still have ceilings, sometimes vaulted as in VI.7.20-2 (Fig. 117). Indol and methylindol (also known as skatole), which are responsible for the characteristic smell of faeces, must have lingered in the air. Urine decomposition must have contributed to this with the smell of ammonia.

During a survey of the latrines in Regio VIII in 2006 the latrine of the theatre was studied (Fig. 118). Normally entry to it is discouraged by two ropes. These had been pulled out of the wall and use had been made of the latrine by tourists, not only to deposit rubbish but also to urinate and carry out other activities. Four large plastic bags were filled with unmentionable material before the photograph was taken, and the stench was unbearable,

118. Latrine by the entrance to the large theatre from the triangular forum.

producing coughing and retching. The place itself is dark with two small windows, and despite the fact that there would have been water running through the drain to remove the excreta, it must have been very unpleasant in Roman times.

Occasionally evidence of wooden pegs can be found inserted into a wall beside or behind the latrine. Perhaps hung upon these were garlands of flowers or sweet-smelling herbs.

The Romans did comment about smells. Cicero writes

> *Atque ut in aedificiis architecti avertunt ab oculis naribusque dominorum ea quae profluentia necessario taetri essent aliquid habitura, sic natura res similis procul amandavit a sensibus.*

> Just as architects relegate the drains of houses to the rear, away from the eyes and nose of the masters, since otherwise they would inevitably be somewhat offensive, so nature has banished the corresponding organs of the body far away from the neighbourhood of the senses. (Cicero *De Natura Deorum* II.lvi.141, tr. Rackham)

Although this implies only that that the smell of human excreta would be offensive to an élite Roman, it may also apply to smells from other drains.

108

8. Dirt, smell and culture

Cicero is speaking as one of a small select group who may have had some degree of control of their personal environment.

Columella states, of the siting of the wine room in the house:

Quae summota procul esse debet a balineis, furno, stercilino reliquisque immunditiis taetrum odorem spirantibus

It should be far removed from the baths, oven, dunghill and other filthy places which give off a foul odour (Columella *On Agriculture* I.6.11, tr. Harrison Boyd Ash)

He also comments on the best place for bee hives:

Si villae situs ita conpetit, non est dubitandum quin aedificio iunctum apiarium maceria circumdemus, sed in ea parte quae tetris latrinae stercilinique et a balinei libera est odoribus

If the situation of the farm permits, we ought not to hesitate to join the apiary to a building and surround it with a wall, but it must be on the side of the house which is free from the foul odours which come from the latrines, the dunghill and the bathroom (Columella *On Agriculture* IX.5.1, tr. Forster and Heffner).

Once again it is the smell which stimulates the comment, but note also the reference in both cases to the baths. Seneca, writing about Scipio Africanus who had lived 250 years previously, comments that he didn't bathe every day and people of that time washed only their arms and legs on a daily basis. Seneca goes on, 'Of course someone will say "Surely they were very smelly men?" ' His retort is 'And what do you think they smelled of? – Of the army, of farm work and of manliness' (see Shelton 1998: 311).

The character Ergasilus in Plautus' *Captivi* comments:

Tum piscatores, qui praebent populo pisces foetidos,
qui advehuntur quadrupedanti crucianti cantherio,
quorum odos subbasilicanos omnes abigit in forum.

Then fishmongers that travel around on a jogging, jolting gelding, offer folk stale fish so strong it drives every last lounger in the arcade out into the forum. (Plautus *Captivi* 813, tr. Nixon)

Of course it must be realised that modern concepts of foul smell are culturally influenced and what may today be described as 'rank' or 'disgusting' may not have evoked the same response in Roman times. However, we do know from the writings of Martial that the odour of stale urine was considered extremely unpleasant. The excavation of the Roman site at Saint-Romain-en-Galle revealed an amphora at a street corner (Brissaud 2003). This would have been an ideal place for the collection of urine, which was used in the fulling industry. Did people urinate directly into these, or were they there only to collect the contents of chamber pots? The lower half of an amphora was discovered hanging from a wall by the House of Julius Polybius in Pompeii (Brion 1960: 136), and although we have no scientific evidence, as yet, that these were for urine, there are many references to similar finds throughout the Roman world (see Bradley 2002: 30 n. 85).

The smell emanating from urine deposited in such receptacles as these and left standing for a while would have had a quite obnoxious ammoniacal quality. The following epigram, as well as commenting strongly on the personal odour of Thais, also suggests that these pots were subject to breakage, polluting the street.

> *tam male Thais olet quam non fullonis avari*
> *testa vetus media, sed modo fracta via,*
> *non ab amore recens hircus, non ora leonis,*
> *non detracta cani Transtiberina cutis,*
> *pullus abortivo nec cum putrescit in ovo*
> *amphora corrupto nec vitiata garo*

> Thais smells worse than the veteran crock of a stingy fuller
>   recently broken in the middle of the road,
> or a billy goat fresh from his amours, or a lion's mouth,
>   or a hide from beyond the Tiber,
> or a chicken rotting in an aborted egg,
>   or a jar polluted with putrid garum.
>
> Martial VI.93, tr. Shackleton Bailey

Most human beings develop relatively neutral or positive reactions and feelings to the smells produced by their own bodies but at the same time tend to have negative attitudes to the odours of the bodies of others (Loudon 1977: 162). Masking of body odour by the use of perfumes, which by their characteristics and intensity make it difficult or impossible to detect the offensive smell, was practised in Roman times just as it is today (Dague 1972: 591). Martial makes comparisons with other odours which were obviously considered exceedingly offensive at the time, including the smell from tanneries. Surprisingly, the fulleries in Pompeii, where urine was used, are in general closely adjacent to large élite properties. Examples of this are the *fullonica* I.10.5-6, situated next door to the House of Menander, and another, VI.15.3, next door but one to the House of the Vettii (Moeller 1976).

It is likely that the owners of the large houses had financial interests in these workplaces, and perhaps the enclosed nature of the buildings limited the spread of the odour. There is also the probability that clothes which had been cleaned by the fullers retained the smell of urine to which even the rich became accustomed (see Bradley 2002: 36). Perhaps even the purple stripe of the highest social class smelt foul. Strabo comments on the smell from the dyeworks in Tyre where *Murex* shells were processed to make Tyrian purple (*Geography* XVI.2.23), and Pliny the Elder comments upon the price paid for the shells and the smell of their processing:

> *Sed unde conchyliis pretia, quis virus grave in fuco, color austerus in glauco, et irascenti similis mari?*

> But what is the cause for the prices paid for purple shells, which have an unhealthy odour when used for dye, and a gloomy tinge in their radiance, resembling an angry sea (Pliny the Elder *Natural History* IX.127, tr. Jones)

Martial suggests that a woman, Philaenis, wore purple to disguise her own smell (compare his comments on Thais, above):

> *Tinctis murice vestibus quod omni*
> *et nocte utitur et die Philaenis,*
> *non est ambitiosa nec superba:*
> *delectatur odore, non colore.*

> Philaenis wears purple-dyed garments every night and day, but she is not ostentatious or haughty; she likes the odour, not the colour. (Martial IX.62, tr. Shackleton Bailey)

A painting from a latrine in Pompeii (IX.7.22) shows the goddess Fortuna next to a man between two snakes, apparently advising the person entering the toilet to beware of the danger of the pollution of defecation: *Cacator cave malu(m)*. Opinions differ about this interpretation, however, and it seems reasonable to suggest that the goddess and snakes may be there to guard the person from the evil eye while involved in what was recognised as a potentially dangerous act, or as protectors of cleanliness (see Magaldi 1932; Koloski-Ostrow 2000, 292; also Mygind 1921, 289 on snake figures on walls and altars to ward off evil). This warning is replicated several times in Pompeii (see Chapter 10 below, pp. 144-5). In the *Satyricon* Trimalchio explains his will to his guests and discusses his tomb. He ends by saying that he will appoint one of his freemen to mount guard on the tomb so that it will not come to any harm and, in particular, to ensure that people do not make a beeline to shit against it (Petronius *Satyricon* 71)

Even that epitome of Roman cleanliness, the baths, was probably not as hygienic a place as might be supposed (see Fagan 2002), with Celsus advising that:

> *Balneum quoque, dum parum vulnus purum est, inter res infestissimus est. Nam id et umidum et sordidum reddit, ex quibus ad cancrum transitus esse consuevit.*

Bathing, too, while the wound is not yet clean, is one of the worst things to do; for this makes the wound both wet and dirty and there is a tendency for gangrene to occur. (Celsus *De Medicina* V.26.28, tr. Spencer)

In the *Satyricon* (117) the companions hire a man as a porter. When he falls out with them for walking too quickly, not only does he swear at them but he immediately lifts up his leg and fills the street with the noise and odour of a fart. No doubt this was a source of humour to the reader, but it also conveys the social offence produced by the noxious vapour. However, after hearing about a man who had died, allegedly by being obsessively modest about breaking wind, the Emperor Claudius planned to legalise farting at the table (Suetonius *Claudius* 32). This, no doubt, would have pleased Fabullus, the husband of Bassa:

Infantem secum semper tua Bassa, Fabulle,
  collocat et lusus deliciasque vocat,
et, quo mireris magis, infantaria non est.
  Ergo quid in causa est? Pedere Bassa solet.

Your Bassa, Fabullus, always puts a baby by her side and calls it darling and pet; and, for your greater wonderment, she is no baby lover. So what is her reason? Bassa has a habit of farting. (Martial IV.87, tr. Shackleton Bailey)

Another indicator of what was considered an obnoxious smell is, again, to do with personal odour.

Auriculum Mario graviter miraris olere.
  Tu facis hoc: garris, Nestor, in auriculam

You are surprised that Marius' ear smells disagreeably. That is your doing. You chatter, Nestor, in his ear. (Martial III.28, tr. Shackleton Bailey)

A discharge from the ear can be caused by an infection due to *Pseudomonas pyocyanea*. There is universal agreement among those who work in ENT departments of hospitals that this has a particularly disagreeable smell. This suggests that, even though 'the adaptive capability of human culture can, within limitations, attach positive or negative notions to certain smells, thereby making them acceptable or even desirable', some odours are likely to be judged unpleasant by all and sundry – whatever cultural background (Bartosiewicz 2003: 190).

Smells from the kitchen may be assumed to have been appetising. Indeed Juvenal writes that a pleasant cooking smell could enslave clients to their patrons.

tu tibi liber homo et regis conviva videris:
captum te nidore suae putat ille culinae

8. Dirt, smell and culture

You think yourself a free man and the guest of a public figure; he thinks, and he is not far wrong, that you have been captured by the savoury odours of his kitchen. (Juvenal V.161-2, tr. Ramsay)

Seneca, however, deprecates the pollution and smell from Rome's collective kitchens.

Ut primum gravitatem urbis excessi et illum odorem culinarum fumantium quae motae quicquid pestiferi vaporis obferunt cum pulvere effundunt, protinus mutatam valitudinem sensi.

As soon as I escaped from the oppressive atmosphere of the city, and from that awful odour of reeking kitchens, which, when in use, pour forth a ruinous mess of steam and soot, I perceived at once that my health was mending. (Seneca *Epistulae* 104.6, tr. Gummere)

Throughout the city of Pompeii there were shops and bars selling food, some of which was cooked there. Many of these are adjacent to the houses where the rich people lived. Perhaps Seneca's comment did not apply to Pompeii, where the street odour of hot food may have been rather more appetising.

A further problem may have been the odour from cesspits. Those in the street, and there were many, were probably covered by the sidewalk or by wooden covers. This may have helped to contain the smell. But hot conditions with high humidity and low air circulation, particularly in the summer months, are likely to have increased the noxious odour in the streets (Dague 1972: 592). It is possible that toilets with cesspits within the home may have had a simple wooden lid – something akin perhaps to the ones from Thorpe Hall near Stowmarket, which may date from the early eighteenth century (Lambton 1978: fig. 17). A diagram in the report on the latrine in the Roman Fort at Bearsden indicates that each of the nine seats had a separate lid, the annotation stating that these would lift off to facilitate cleaning (Breeze 1984: 57).

The inorganic gases resulting from biological activity in cesspits include hydrogen sulphide and ammonia, both of which are malodorous (Dague 1972: 583). The physiology of the olfactory receptors that are given an interpretation of smell by the brain is affected by the amount of stimulus received by the nerve endings in the nasal mucosa. A heavy continuous stimulus results in exhaustion of the neuronal discharge, and the brain no longer receives the signal identifying the odour. It is therefore possible that the noxious smells from tanneries, drains and cesspits would be less of an inconvenience to those who worked within these areas and probably to those in the immediate neighbourhood. Nevertheless, these odours would no doubt be offensive to visitors.

There are always problems when attempting to use analogy as evidence in support of a particular archaeological interpretation. Just because the stench from the river Thames in 1858 was referred to, even in Parliament, as the 'great stink' (Halliday 1999: 71), this does not mean that the Pompeians objected to what might have been a similar odour from the river Sarno, into which some of the effluent from the city drained.

There is also a common belief that the streets of medieval London were polluted, not just by excreta but by other forms of rubbish. How much did this impinge on the daily lives of the inhabitants? An examination of *Letter Books,* the written sources, suggests that although there were problems, the actual degree of environmental pollution was not as severe as has been surmised (Sabine 1934, 1970).

Two further examples may help to judge the state of affairs in Pompeii. During the early seventeenth century the Florentine health magistrates took steps to cleanse the towns and cities of their area, issuing ordinances regarding the clearing of rubbish heaps, sewers and stagnant water – all of which produced foul odours (Cipolla 1992). Miasma (a noxious smell) was considered a health hazard that contributed to infectious diseases, especially the plague. In his report of 1607, the master mason Lucini wrote: 'Castelfranco is pervaded by the stench emanating from certain places where sewage runs which are open and lack cesspits. In Bientina things are very badly arranged because the [chamber] pots, all inadequately set just below the commodes, let the waste run out through gaps in the walls and fall into certain narrow alleys between the houses into which the inhabitants throw all the dirt and rubbish from their houses. The result is a stench and filth so awful that it is quite impossible to live there' (Cipolla 1992: 16). It was not only human excrement that contributed to this smell. In Bientina 'they keep the manure from their stables outside on the road next to the walls, where it rots and stinks terribly'. In Santa Maria a Monte, as elsewhere, other animals contributed to the problem. 'Some reduction must be made to the number of pigs, because nearly every household has one and their sties stink to high heaven!' (Cipolla 1992: 19). To add to the flavour there were other unpleasant smells from butchers' waste, rope making, tanning and linen retting (Cipolla 1992: 23). Although these comments were made by members of an administrative hierarchy, it is almost certain that the towns and cities of upper central Italy at the time were unpleasant places in which to live and work.

Just prior to the French Revolution the environment of Paris, according to the sanitary reformers of the time, was such that workers were endangered by gases emanating from cesspools and had to be protected against suffocation (Corbin 1986: 27). A hierarchy of exhalations and vapours that emanated from cesspools was described. This system corresponded to a progressive ageing and corruption of faecal matter with first the odour of fresh excrement, then the odour of the latrine, then the odour expelled by the pits and finally the odour of cesspool cleansing (Hallé 1785: 77). The epicentre of the stench in Paris was the Montfaucon area, where sewage reservoirs and slaughterhouses stood side by side. However, although sewage was discharged into the river Seine, the purity of the river was not impaired since it was constantly being refreshed.

This brief exploration into the attitudes to odour of the Romans and other peoples leaves many gaps in our understanding. Certainly, olfactory physiology is capable of recognising a variety of different sensations and these are interpreted according to the expectations and cultural background of the recipient. Perhaps the inhabitants of Pompeii were resigned to the smell from their cesspits, knowing that there was little they could do about it, or indeed not knowing what to do about it, or was that why they moved their toilets upstairs?

Water supply, usage and disposal

In the ancient world water fulfilled a multitude of functions: utilitarian, religious, social, symbolic and industrial. At one end of the spectrum it provided a resource for transportation of goods; at the other a necessity for life itself, drinking water. The strategies of its usage and consumption reflected the size and complexity of the urbanisation of a community.

The Romans were fully aware of the importance of water in their lives. Celsus differentiated a range of quality, from rainwater, which he called the lightest, to marsh water, the heaviest (Celsus *De Medicina* II.18.12). Pliny the Elder also discussed quality, although he found difficulty in accepting rainwater or snow as the best because he recognised the presence of pollutants from the air in both (*Natural History* XXXI.21/2).

Household water could be obtained by digging wells down to the water table or by tapping springs. In Pompeii the wells were dug through the lava spur upon which the city stands. Most of these appear to have been situated in public places, providing water for everybody, although some houses had wells of their own. Rainwater was collected, usually falling from the *compluvium* into a gutter in the *impluvium* and thence into a cistern which would provide storage for periods of time when rainfall was scarce (Vitruvius *On Architecture* VI.14). Occasionally narrow bore pipes might bring the rainwater directly off the roof directly into the cistern in VI.16.28 (Fig. 119).

Cisterns abounded. At some time around the fourth century BCE, waterproof cement lining was invented which prevented seepage out from, and contamination into, the cisterns. These varied in size. For example the one in the House of the Painted Capitals in Pompeii measures 12.5 x 2.2 m and was 2.7 m high; it would have held about 69,000 litres of water (Sear 1994). During periods of heavy rainfall the cisterns would fill and overflow; the water then ran out through drains under the door thresholds into the streets, helping to clean them (Fig. 120).

A desire to imitate Rome in its usage of water for public and private display (fountains and fish and swimming pools, etc.) led to the construction of an aqueduct to Pompeii at the time of the early Empire. This aqueduct provided a major change in the supply of water, bringing it to a *castellum* at the highest point of the city from where it was distributed, using lead pipes, to public fountains, workplaces and private houses. This was carried out via a complex tower and siphon system with taps to control supply. The piped water gave new opportunities for aquatic display within houses and the mere sight of this expensive luxury, which for private

119. Narrow bore down pipe going directly into a cistern, VI.16.28.

consumption had to be paid for, pouring out through the overflow drains, would signify the élite status of the householder and his apparent disregard for the expense. Despite this apparent accessibility to piped water, there is little evidence to suggest that it was brought to kitchens for drinking and cooking.

Rome, also on a sloping site, had a similar type of street cleaning. Frontinus comments on overflow water from reservoirs and fountains:

Nam necesse est ex castellis aliquam partem aquae effluere, cum hoc pertineat non solum ad urbis nostrae salubritatem, sed etiam ad utilitatem cloacarum abluendarum.

For there must necessarily be some overflow from the reservoirs, this being proper not only for the health of our city, but also for use in the flushing of the sewers. (Frontinus *Aqueducts* II.3, tr. Bennett).

120. Drain from the House of the Vestals into the Vicolo di Narciso.

The water here is being used to flush the streets. What evidence is there for the use of water to flush the toilets?

First, there is the presence of sloping tiled floors. Although only four of the latrines found in Pompeii Regio VI.1 have tiling, most of the toilets in Pompeii have sloping tiled floors (Fig. 121). This would appear to be confirmatory evidence that water was used as a cleansing agent. Perhaps the sloping tiles were there purely to direct urine if males were urinating standing in front of the toilet seat. This explanation presupposes that Roman males urinated standing up.

A number of latrines in Pompeii have foot-rests, underneath which the water would flow into the cesspits. Fig. 122 shows one such, with the tiled floor passing beneath the stone foot-rest and an unusual sloping area chute leading to an exit hole in the wall for excreta to be washed into the cesspit in the street. In a number of kitchens, as well as the slope into the latrine, there is another exit hole to take excess water through the wall into the street, as shown in Fig. 123. To the left of the hole in the wall to the sidewalk outside, is the solid cooking surface, above which is a vertical mark on the wall suggesting a wooden divide between the kitchen and the latrine.

It is most probable that not all tiled surfaces led into latrines. In a work area at VII.3.3 there is an interesting feature which might be for rubbish disposal (Fig. 124). Some degree of modern reconstruction makes interpretation rather difficult, but it is visible from the street making it unlikely to be a latrine.

121. Tiled floor in workshop, VII.15.4.

122. Drainage under footrest into chute and exit through wall drain, clothing workshop, VI.11.6,13.

123. Kitchen latrine with tile exit pipe into street, House of Cipius Pamphilus Felix, VII.6.37.

124. Possible industrial waste disposal, Workshop of C. Memmius, VII.3.3.

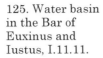

125. Water basin
in the Bar of
Euxinus and
Iustus, I.11.11.

Next there is the presence (or in VI.1 the absence) of water tanks. It has been said that private toilets usually had some sort of water basin (Jansen 20002: 60). Not one of the systems in VI.1 had such a provision. In fact, hardly any toilets in Pompeii have associated water tanks, a rarity being seen in I.11.11 (Fig. 125). This is a latrine which has its entry from the garden. It is probably a late addition to the house facilities and may originally have been a woodshed. The room is decorated with a black dado topped by a red line, making it one of the few well decorated latrines in Pompeii (Jansen 1993).

In the majority of cases water would have been brought to the latrine in buckets. Repetitive use of a latrine in a *taberna,* for example, might require regular flushing with water from a bowl or bucket and perhaps use of the water as a sponge cleanser. That process would necessarily pollute the water, which might occasion it to be renewed regularly with buckets from an outside source, the most likely being the local street fountain.

In the Villa at Oplontis water for the latrine is supplied from a large cistern which has two exit holes (Fig. 126). The lower of these supplies the sewer and could empty the whole contents of the cistern if necessary. The upper exit drain, for fresh water from the cistern, supplied the washing trough and could be fed using a bucket.

Niche toilets on upper storeys (see below) would have required flushing to keep the pipes clear (Jansen 1997: 12ff.). Most modern authors have assumed that flushing with water did take place and that it was primarily for hygienic purposes. As has already been indicated, there is no doubt that, in addition, the bacterial decomposition of the excreta in the cesspits would have been accelerated by the persistent addition of

drain for
personal washing

drain for sewer

126. The corner of the cistern of the latrine at Oplontis showing two drainage holes.

water, especially in the warm climatic conditions of the city of Pompeii during the summer months.

Niches are also found accommodating ground floor latrines (Fig. 127). Here there are no tiled surfaces because the excrement falls vertically.

Piped water was, in fact, supplied to a small number of toilets. '... two toilets had running water; in the toilet of the House of the Silver Wedding, a tap is attached in the wall (no longer to be seen since the whole latrine room has collapsed): and in the House of the Faun, a hole for a pipe can be seen next to the toilet seat and a groove for a pipe cut out in the outer wall of the house' (Jansen 2001: 40 n. 42). Another author states 'I have thus far found no evidence for piped water into a kitchen or latrine, except in the latrines associated with the baths in the House of the Centenary and in the House of Julia Felix' (Jashemski 1979: 53). There is no clarification about the actual use of the water for flushing the latrine. At this point the question must be asked: If water was worth piping to one or two latrines and so much of it was being put down latrines, why are there not more water pipes in or near latrines? Cheap labour could have brought water into houses from the street fountains but installation of a lead pipe supply would have been expensive. This suggests that the use of running water was a social behaviour relating to the rich sections of Roman society.

To clarify this a little, there is a latrine in the House of L. Caecilius

127. Niche latrine,
House of Diana,
VIII.3.16.

Communis (VII.13.14) which had water running across the room in front
of the latrine, to exit through the wall to the north via a terracotta pipe
(Fig. 128). The southern end of this pipe abuts the southern wall of the
room. The northern end of the pipe runs out through the north wall and
its contents would have passed down the groove in the kerbstone and
dropped onto the road surface from where it percolated through into the
cesspit below the road (Fig. 129). The pipe carrying water across the room
in front of the toilet could easily have been diverted into the toilet.

In the south wall a few centimetres directly above the end of the drain there
is a small hole approximately 4 cm in diameter. This hole is 22 cm above the
base of the drain, not really high enough to rest a sizeable bucket under,
though a modern Italian bucket is only about 22 cm high. On the other side
of the wall is a lead pipe entering the wall (Fig. 130). This appears to be
ascending from the floor below, though there is no positive evidence for where
it comes from. Piped water is, in fact, entering the house only a few metres
away. The lead pipe crosses the street and ascends up a groove in the
kerbstone to enter the house at its north-east corner (Fig. 131).

128. Latrine showing water channel running across the floor in front of the toilet, House of L. Caecilius Communis, VII.13.14.

129. Water pipe emerging through wall with groove in kerbstone, House of L. Caecilius Communis, VII.13.14.

130. Lead pipe going into wall from south to deliver water to latrine room, House of L. Caecilius Communis, VII.13.14.

131. Groove in kerbstone for lead pipe coming from street and going through wall into house, House of L. Caecilius Communis, VII.13.14.

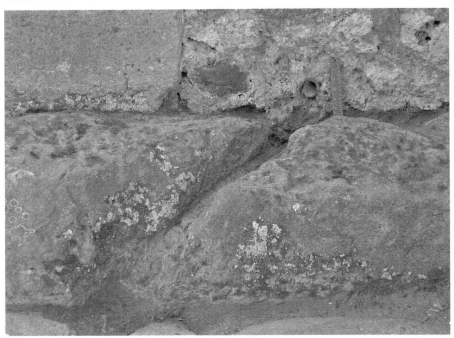

9. Water supply, usage and disposal

It would appear that from the Augustan period, when piped water was available for display in the fountains of the élite houses, this particular house used this water supply system to provide intermittent running water through the latrine room. Since it was running directly onto the street it would seem likely that cleansing of the toilet itself was considered unnecessary, but the tiles could have been washed from the supply. Fig. 132 shows the lead piping in the sidewalk diagonally across from VII.13.14. This comes from the fountain supply up the street to the north. Unfortunately this pipe is no longer present since it was removed for modern resurfacing of the sidewalk in 2008.

Finally, there is evidence that the waste water of the *caldarium* of the House of the Faun was used to flush the latrine in a room south of the *caldarium* (De Haan 2001: 44), and also that the water from the pool of the House of Julia Felix was relayed through the multi-seat latrine to wash the effluent into a cesspit (Parslow 2000: 201 and plan 203). In the House of the Grand Duke, VII.4.56, the toilet is situated beyond the kitchen at the southern end of the property. A pipe runs from the gutter of the peristyle through the kitchen and into the toilet, and it has been suggested that this is a way of disposing of the water from the fountain in the peristyles (Sear 2004: 162). Similarly the latrine in room 26 of the House of Menander was flushed by water from a sink in the kitchen (room 27) to

132. Lead piping running down sidewalk diagonally opposite VII.13.14.

the north. It is also thought that down pipes carried rainwater to flush latrines in both I.10.2,3 and the House of the Craftsman, I.10.7 (Ling 1997: 92f.). Unfortunately there is insufficient information about the diameter of these down pipes and they may have serviced latrines on the upper storey.

Mau shows a drain from the large swimming tank in the Central Baths passing to the public latrine, presumably to act as a sluicing system. However, he does not indicate the sewer drainage from that latrine (Mau 1902: 209). Although no excavation has been carried out to confirm this, it is believed that the drainage from this latrine is into a large cesspit (De Haan, personal communication). In Ostia the provision of latrines in one *insula* (V.ii) during the mid-fourth century CE includes one latrine in V.ii.8 which has an 'ingenious flushing system' using the water from a *nymphaeum* nearby (Boersma 1996: 156). In this insula 'all the houses which were provided with latrines had water facilities' (Boersma 1996: 159). Although this is dealing with only one *insula*, it would appear that as far as the usage of water for flushing was concerned, little progress had been made in almost two hundred years.

Hadrian's Villa at Tivoli, built over forty years after the destruction of Pompeii, demonstrates that within a huge complex of buildings the latrines varied from multi- to single-seat facilities (Jansen 2003). Several of the single-seat latrines were flushed with rainwater brought down from the roofs by pipes which discharged into the collector beneath the toilet seat. In some other single-seat latrines overflow water from adjacent *nymphaea* was used to flush the systems (Jansen 2003: 145). This certainly suggests that the technology was available if desired.

The earthquake of 62 CE caused major damage to the city of Pompeii. One of the facilities affected was the water supply, and recent excavations in the House of the Vestals show that the house underwent major changes to enable its owners to cope with this loss. Research is required to confirm that some latrines were modified so that less water was used to flush the tiles. In Pompeii only one down pipe can be seen, made of lead (IX.5.1) (Fig. 133). This does not appear to be coming from an upper storey latrine, nor does it appear to go into a latrine. Perhaps, following the earthquake, a section of the road piping was ripped up and re-used as a down pipe from the roof. Unfortunately it has been removed so no further investigation can be carried out.

In the Roman world the disposal of human effluent was intricately linked with cesspits and sewers. In Rome the drainage system of the city was begun in the sixth century BCE when the Cloaca Maxima was constructed.

> And the sewers, vaulted with close-fitting stones, have in some places left room enough even for wagons loaded with hay to pass through them. And water is brought into the city through the aqueducts in such quantities that veritable rivers flow through the city and the sewers (Strabo *Geography* V.3.7-8, tr. Jones)

133. Vertical lead pipe, IX.5.1.

The original purpose of the Cloaca Maxima was to drain the marshy area which became the Forum Romanum (Hodge 1992: 333; Dodge 2000: 193). All the side channels that emptied into the Cloaca Maxima from the Forum Augustum to the Tiber belonged to the streets or public buildings – none to private dwellings – and were added later, after the system, which was originally an open ditch, had been paved over. Cesspits abounded, but only one, in a building ascribed to the Praetorians, appeared to Lanciani to be worthy of comment and excavation. This demonstrated an intricate labyrinth of 'sewers' which all ended in a large 'black hole' with a vaulted roof and no exit. Lanciani identified this as a repository within which the corpses of those killed in popular uprisings or as victims of secret assassinations were left to decay (Lanciani 1873).

The practice of incorporating underground drains was by no means the rule in the Roman world. It certainly did not apply to Smyrna:

> But there is one error, not a small one, in the work of the engineers, that when they paved the streets they did not give them underground drain-

129

age. Instead filth covers the surface and particularly during rains when the cast-off filth is discharged upon the streets. (Strabo *Geography* XIV.1.37, tr. Jones)

By contrast, in the city of Timgad, founded by Trajan in 100 CE, 'all the streets had well built sewers beneath them' (Haverfield 1913: 112). In Lincoln, founded *c.* 75 CE, 'all the principal streets of the upper town seem to have possessed stone built sewers big enough for a boy to walk along; into them fed smaller drains from private houses' (Frere 1967: 245). At Verulamium there was a similar sized sewer from the forum to the river carrying effluent from a public latrine and private houses (Frere 1967: 246). In Herculaneum the 'early' town had latrines connected to cesspits. However an opportunity presented itself for the removal of latrine waste directly into the drain, which ran towards the sea down the centre of a main street, associated with the later construction of a large bath. There was also a similar drain which provided for the waste from the latrines of a large 'apartment block' (Jansen 1992). In Ostia there were no cesspits and a complex sewer system disposed of the refuse (Van Dam & Versloot 1995: 15).

Mau discusses the surface drainage system of Pompeii, noting that 'there were covered conduits to carry the surface water of the forum' and that these ran 'under the Strada del Scuole to the south and the Via Marina to the west'. In addition he states that there were exit storm drains at the west ends of the Vico dei Soprastanti and the Strada di Nola. His final comment involves a drain which he says 'leads from Abbondanza Street where it is crossed by Stabian Street toward the south' (Mau 1902: 229).

In his publication of work carried out in Pompeii in November 1900, Sogliano (1990) was more explicit. He explains that, given the sloping nature of the terrain, water flowed from the upper part of the city to the lower, and that besides rain water the overflows from the fountains and from the houses contributed to the flow. Because of this, he comments, 'from time to time, in appropriate places it was conveyed in underground drains that lead out of the built up areas.' Here he particularly mentions a junction between drains uniting at the western junction of VI.4 and the Via Nola (Via delle Terme) and then going south taking water from VI.1, V1.2, VI.3 and VI.4.

Although he is not totally explicit, Sogliano says that another drain runs under the northern aspect of VII.15. The full extent of this was not known at the time since the buildings of the western *insula* had not been excavated. He then goes on to say that the forum had drains on the east, west and south sides leaving down the Via Marina between the Basilica and the Temple of Apollo. He further notes that other 'minor courses' joined this (but were only partly excavated). Most interestingly, he describes a huge cistern under the south side of the forum, *c.* 50 x 2.5 m. He says that the water flowing into this would be less impure than that from other areas since the forum was inaccessible to animal-drawn vehicles. He describes a separate series of drains running under the Via Abbondanza, one part passing south under the Via Stabiae to leave the city, the other apparently going under the large theatre towards the north-west corner of the Gladiators' School and finally passing out through the city wall. Again he notes that 'a number of water courses and foul waste water drains join this', some of which 'appear to have been made after the original construction – the intention of which, at first was the single purpose of collecting rainwater'. It is important to note that at no time in his paper does Sogliano suggest that latrines are discharging into these drains.

Further work by Arthur (1986: 37) expands the understanding of the drainage in the forum area. He states that 'during the late Republic the forum was equipped with a central sewer with collateral culverts. In Imperial times run-off from the forum was directed through a series of holes cut in the travertine blocks lining the square into a number of conduits which converged with the main sewer to sluice beneath the Via dell' Abbondanza or the Via Marina.' He regrets 'for safety reasons, being unable to draw up a plan of the entire system' but states that there was 'a sewer draining the Temple of Apollo and another, now sealed off, which commenced in front of the House of Triptolemus'. He also found evidence of earlier, minor, drainage systems using amphorae.

The practice of incorporating water drainage channels into latrines, especially from baths, had very practical advantages, including using the waste water for flushing purposes (Dodge 2000: 191). That there were such channels is confirmed by Eschebach in his description of the Stabian Baths (Eschebach 1979). Not only does he describe the sewer as starting from the centre of the rear seating row, but he shows it running south towards the Palaestra and then being joined by other drains from the baths, eventually going into the main drain in the Via Abbondanza. Sogliano also mentions the opening of this drain as it exits from the Stabian Baths. It had not been emptied of its contents but was said to be different from the others in that it was made of cemented bricks with heavy calcareous deposits (Sogliano 1900: 599).

10

Who used these toilets?

Do the Romans tell us much about using the toilet? What evidence do we have? Whether our data accrues from artistic impressions, artefacts or writings, there will be factors influencing the weight which can be accorded to the evidence. Ancient authors had certain biases as a result of the culture of their time. The position they occupied within society, and the readership at which they aimed, greatly influenced all aspects of their writings. The following collection of Greek and Roman writings on excrement, latrines and toilet utensils reflects a viewpoint that is almost completely masculine and élitist.

A red-figure wine jug by the Oinokles Painter, *c.* 470 BCE, shows a 'drunken man' urinating into a vessel held by a slave (Fig. 134). The young man is holding a long-handled implement, perhaps a rake, and suspended from his shoulders is a basket. Is he collecting urine and perhaps manure?

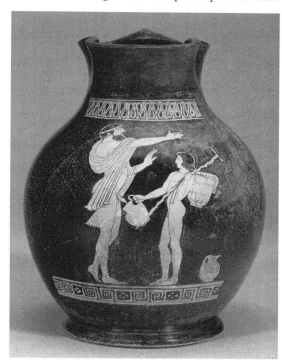

134. Red-figure wine jug by the Oinokles Painter. Getty Museum.

Hesiod gives advice to men about when and where to urinate:

> Do not stand upright facing the sun when you make water, but remember to do this when he has set and towards his rising. And do not make water as you go, whether on the road or off the road, and do not uncover yourself: the nights belong to the blessed gods. A scrupulous man who has a wise heart sits down or goes to the wall of an enclosed court. (*Works and Days* 727-2, tr. Most)

There are a number of classical references to chamber pots. Athenaeus of Naucratis says:

> They (the Sybarites) were the first to invent chamber pots which they carried to their drinking parties. (Athenaeus V.12.519b, tr. Gulick)

In Roman literature chamber pots are referred to as *matellae, lasanae* or *dolia curta*. An enlightening graffito was scratched on a wall in Pompeii at VIII.7.6:

> *Mi(n)ximus in lecto fateor, peccavimus hospes*
> *Si dices quare: nulla matella fuit.*

> Dear Host; We admit we've pissed the bed. 'Why?' You ask. Because you didn't give us a chamber pot (*CIL* 4.4957, tr. Pascal)

In a similar vein:

> *puri saepe lacum propter si ac dolia curta*
> *somno devincti credunt se extollere vestem,*
> *totius umorem saccatum corpori fundunt*

> Boys (innocents), often when held fast in sleep, if they think they are lifting up their garments beside a basin or refuse pot, pour forth all the filtered liquid of their bodies. (Lucretius *De Rerum Natura* IV.1026-9, tr. Rouse)

Martial has three epigrams relating to the use, by males, of vessels as chamber pots.

> *digiti crepantis signa novit eunuchus*
> *et delicatae sciscitator urinae*
> *domini bibentis ebrium regit penem*

> The eunuch knows the signal of his snapping fingers and probes the coy urine, guiding a tipsy penis as his master drinks. (Martial III.82, tr. Shackleton Bailey)

Note that the chamber pot is only inferred. Also reminiscent of the above graffiti is the following:

134

10. Who used these toilets?

Dum poscor crepitu digitorum et verna moratur,
  O quotiens paelex culcita facta mea est!

While I am summoned with a snap of the fingers, and the slave delays, oh how often has the pillow been my rival! (Martial XIV.119, tr. Shackleton Bailey)

This is a comment, ostensibly by the chamber pot itself, on the fact that if it is not brought, the man will urinate into a pillow. Again:

Cum peteret seram media iam nocte matellam
  arguto madidus pollice Panaretus,
Spoletina data est sed quam siccaverat ipse,
...
Ille fide summa testae sua vina remensus
  reddidit oenophori pondera plena sui.

When tipsy Panaretus snapped his thumb for a late chamber-pot (it was already midnight) he was handed a Spoletine flagon, one which he had drained himself ... with complete accuracy he measured the full quantity of wine back to the jar. (Martial VI.89, tr. Shackleton Bailey)

Apparently Panaretus is not the only one looking for a flagon.

... dum eunt, nulla est in angiporto amphora, quam non impleant, quippe qui vesicam plenam vini habeant

... as they go, there is no amphora in the alley that they do not fill, since they have a bladder full of wine (Macrobius *Saturnalia* 3.15.15, tr. Pascal)

It can be seen from this last epigram that, on occasion, any receptacle could be considered suitable for a man to urinate into. This makes Trimalchio's behaviour at the ball game, when he uses a silver urinal, all the more humorous:

Notavimus etiam res novas: nam duo spadones in diversa parte circuli stabant, quorum alter matellam tenebat argenteam ... Trimalchio digitos concrepuit, ad quod signum matellam spado ludenti subiecit. Exonerata ille vesica aquam poposcit ad manus, digitosque paululum adspersos in capite pueri tersit.

We noticed some other unusual features: two eunuchs stood in the circle facing Trimalchio. One was holding a silver chamber pot ... Trimalchio clicked his fingers, and at this signal the eunuch supplied him with the chamber pot, as he continued playing. The host voided his bladder, and, after perfunctorily washing his fingers, wiped them on the slave's hair. (Petronius *Satyricon* 27, tr. Heseltine)

Several questions present themselves: Was the 'perfunctory' washing significant? What did the Romans of the time consider an act of cleanliness after urination? Perhaps, since Trimalchio was of the *nouveau riche*, he had not had an aristocratic upbringing and thus had not been educated to understand the true significance of hygiene (if indeed there was any understanding of hygiene). Is it significant that the chamber pot was made of silver? This may be further ribaldry: if such precious objects were commonplace then surely one, at least, would have been found during excavation of the élite houses in Pompeii. Finally, did he compound his ignorance by drying his hands on his slave's hair, or was this just a straightforward comment, or indeed a humorous comment since lice were common in the hair of slaves? Lice eggs were found in the hair of a pregnant female whose skeleton was discovered, along with others, in the boat sheds at Herculaneum (Capasso 1998).

Items discarded by the rich may have been useful to the poorer classes:

Chias ad communem revocat matellam

He/she retrieves the Chian amphora of the wealthy for use as a common chamber pot (Varro *Menippean Satires* 192.104)

In a discussion about his problem with constipation Trimalchio makes it obvious that chamber pots are not just for urination.

Vel si quid plus venit, omnia feras parata sunt: aqua, lasani et cetera minutalia.

But if the matter is serious everything is ready outside: water, chamber pots, and all the other little comforts. (Petronius *Satyricon* 47, tr. Heseltine)

Petronius has another reference to a chamber pot:

Ab hoc ferculo Trimalchio ad lasanum surrexit.

After this course Trimalchio rose to go to the pot. (Petronius *Satyricon* 41, tr. Heseltine)

It is important to note that he does not go to the latrine. It appears that, despite the prevalence of latrines throughout the towns, an élite person would carry his chamber pot with him on a journey:

obiciet nemo sordes mihi, quas tibi, Tulli,
cum Tiburte via praetorem quinque sequuntur
te pueri, lasanum portantes oenophorumque.

No one will taunt me with meanness, as he does you, praetor Tullius, when on the Tibur road five slaves follow you carrying a commode [chamber pot] and a case of wine. (Horace *Satires* I.vi.107-9, tr. Fairclough)

135. Wooden toilet (reconstruction), Arbeia, Tyne and Wear Museum.

136. Jug from the bottom of a cesspit in the House of the Triclinium, VI.1.1.

It is possible that portable toilets, under which buckets might have been placed, would have looked something like the reproduction in the Tyne and Wear museum at Arbeia (Fig. 135).

Although there are not, as yet, any ceramic typologies relating to chamber pots, the spread of comments from satire to graffito suggests that there was not only a need for such utensils, but that they were available for use in certain situations. The finding of a jug (Fig. 136) which certainly could have been used by a male for urination, at the bottom of a latrine (Hobson 2002), may be only coincidence, since other ceramics including a lamp were found with it, and inevitably it would have been contaminated by urine, but at least it offers an anecdotal answer to this problem and presumably any handy pot could have been used to urinate into.

All these writings ignore the question, what use of chamber pots was made by women? Herodotus says that the Egyptian women 'urinate standing up' (Herodotus 2.35). Fig. 137 shows a woman urinating into a *krater*. The painting is in the internal base of a cup found at Orvieto, which was almost certainly used by men during *symposia*. If this reflects what happened in the Hellenic period, then might not a Roman woman have used a jug? Martial has one epigram referring to a woman, Bassa, and her chamber pot. It would appear that hers is made of gold:

Ventris onus misero, nec te pudet, excipis auro,
  Basse, bibis vitro: carius ergo cacas.

You receive your belly's load, Bassa, in gold – unlucky gold! – and are not ashamed of it. You drink out of glass. So it costs you more to shit. (Martial I.37, tr. Shackleton Bailey)

137. Red-figure painting in an Attic cup of a woman urinating into a krater.

Where did women go when they needed a toilet? Since shops and bars had toilets it is probable that these were used by passers-by. Also in Pompeii there are a number of single rooms opening directly from the street which have been described as latrines. Such a one is off the Via Abbondanza, VII.14.4. The room probably had a door and would have been eminently suitable for a woman (or of course a man) caught in a moment of crisis.

Urine appears to have been viewed by the Romans from two different perspectives, usually as a waste product and pollutant, but sometimes for its industrial worth. When Juvenal wrote in *Satires* I.131 *cuius ad effigiem non tantum meiiere fas est* 'His effigy's only fit for pissing on – or worse', he was making an insulting political comment. What the reference does tell us is that urine in this situation was considered to be a pollutant. This is mirrored in modern times when there is little worse for one's self-image than being publicly spattered with excrement (Clark and Davis 1989: 657). Yet despite its smell and potential to defile socially it had an economic value. In Rome the collection of urine for industrial purposes was taxed by the Emperor Vespasian:

> *Reprehendenti filio Tito, quod etiam urinae vectigal commentus esset, pecuniam ex prima pensione admovit ad nares, sciscitans num odore offenderetur: at illo negante 'Atque' inquit 'e lotio est'.*

> When Titus, his son, found fault with him for contriving this tax on urine, he held a piece of money, from the first payment, to his son's nose asking him whether its odour was offensive to him. When Titus said 'No' he replied 'Yet it comes from urine'. (Suetonius *Vespasian* XXIII.3, tr. Rolfe)

Pliny the Elder notes:

10. Who used these toilets?

[Cameli] urinam fullonibus utillissima esse trabunt ...

They say that the urine [of a camel] is very useful to the fullers ... (Pliny the Elder *Natural History* XXXVIII.26, tr. Jones)

However, there is no evidence of camel bones in the archaeology of Pompeii, and it would seem that the fullers had to make use of the readily available human supply. (Urine was still being collected for fulling mills in the Huddersfield district in the early twentieth century (Crump & Ghorbal 1935: 36).)

Columella recommends human urine as a fertiliser. He says it also improves the flavour and the bouquet of the wine and the fruit.

> *Aptior est tamen serculis hominis urina, quam sex mensibus passus veterscere si vitibus aut pomorum arboribus adhibeas, nullo alio magis fructus exuberat.*

> Better suited to young shoots, however, is human urine; and if you let it age for six months and then apply it to vines or fruit trees, there is nothing that makes them bear more abundantly. (Columella *On Agriculture* II.xiii.3-xiv, tr. Harrison Boyd Ash)

After performing their ablutions, what did Romans wipe themselves with? There are two references to sponges:

> *Nuper in ludo bestiariorum unus e Germanis, cum ad matutina spectacula pararetur, secessit ad exonerandum corpus; nullum aliud illi dabatur sine custode secretum. Ibi lignum id quod ad emundanda obscena adhaerante spongia positum est totum in gulam farsit et interclusis faucibus spiritum elisit.*

> For example a German, who was lately in a training school for wild beast gladiators, was making ready for the morning exhibition. He withdrew in order to relieve himself – the one thing he was allowed to do in secret, and without the presence of a guard. While so engaged he seized a wooden stick tipped with a sponge, which was devoted to the vilest uses. He stuffed it, just as it was, down his throat; thus he blocked his windpipe and choked the breath from his body. (Seneca *Epistulae* 70.19-21,23, tr. Gummere)

This does not necessarily imply that the sponge on the stick was used for personal cleansing; it might have been used to wipe the toilet (or for both purposes).

The second reference comes from Martial:

> *Lauta tamen cena est: fateor, lautissima, sed cras*
> *nil erit, immo hodie, protinus immo nihil,*
> *quod sciat infelix damnatae spongia virgae*
> *vel quicumque canis iunctaque testa viae*

It's a fine dinner: very fine, I confess, but tomorrow it will be nothing, or rather today, or rather a moment from now it will be nothing; a matter for a luckless sponge on a doomed mop stick or for some dog or other, [vomit] or a crock by the roadside to take care of. (Martial XII.48, tr. Shackleton Bailey)

This time the implication is that this utensil was for personal cleansing. Dogs were noted to eat human excrement, and the wayside crock alludes to the collection of urine. Martial does talk about an alternative use for a sponge:

> *Haec tibi sorte datur tergendis spongia mensis*
> *utilis, expresso cum levis imbre tumet*

This sponge is given to you by lot; it is useful for wiping tables, when it becomes light and swells after the water is squeezed out. (Martial XIV.144, tr. Shackleton Bailey)

The mythology which has grown up about the sponge has not been helped by the finding of spicules of the freshwater sponge, *Spongilla lacustris,* in samples from the Church Street Roman Sewer System at York (Buckland 1976: 14). This type of sponge is said to be unsuitable for toilet use because the spicules are hard and *Euspongia officinalis*, the Mediterranean sponge lacks spicules. An alternative suggestion, based on findings at Bearsden fort, is that moss may have been used (Dickson 1979: 441).

The Romans have deservedly earned a reputation for sub-street sewerage systems, but it is important to understand exactly what constituted toilet drains since there is a modern tendency to define a sewer as a drain conveying faecal material. In fact the passage of sewage into pipes flowing under roads in Roman cities was by no means the norm.

The problem with the etymology of the words drain/sewer is not solved by translators. In Bennett's translation of Frontinus, the discussion of the role of water in the health of the city translates the word *cloaca* as sewer, when talking of overflow from the reservoirs being necessary for the flushing of the drainage system. The Roman reader of Frontinus' work would undoubtedly have known what materials were carried in the *cloacae*.

> *Caducam neminem volo ducere nisi qui meo beneficio aut priorum prin-*
> *cipum habent. Nam necesse est ex castellis aliquam partem aquae effluere,*
> *cum hoc pertineat non solum ad urbis nostrae salubritatem, sed etiam ad*
> *utilitatem cloacorum abluendarum.*

I desire that no one shall draw 'lapsed' water except those who have permission to do so by grants from me or preceding sovereigns; for there must necessarily be some overflow from the reservoirs, this being proper not only for the health of our City, but also for use in flushing of the sewers. (Frontinus *Aqueducts of Rome* II.111, tr. Bennett)

In this context the word *cloacorum* is generally descriptive and has no particular relevance to toilet waste.

It is important to try to decide what became of the contents of the cesspits in Pompeii. Columella states:

> *Tria igitur genera stercoris sunt praecipue, quod ex avibus, quod ex hominibus, quod ex pecudibus confit.*

> [There are] three main types of manure: that produced by birds, by human-kind, and by cattle. (Columella *On Agriculture* II.xiv.1, tr. Boyd Ash)

He goes on:

> *Secundum deinde, quod homines faciunt, si et aliis villae purgamentis immisceatur quoniam per se naturae est ferventioris et idcirco terram perurit.*

> Human excrement is second in effectiveness to pigeon dung, if it is mixed with other refuse of the farmstead because by itself it is rather hot and burns the ground. (Columella *On Agriculture* II.xiv.2, tr. Boyd Ash)

Finally, as we saw on p. 100, he recommends that gardeners spread dung, including that from latrines, on their land. Assuming that this was a well-established practice, the contents of cesspits from latrines become valuable commodities and not just waste. Curiously, pampered ladies in Rome swore by a face pack made of the dung of the land lizard (Nutton 1985).

The social status of the people who constructed latrines is commented upon by Juvenal:

> *cedamus patria. vivant Artorius istic*
> *et Catulus, maneant qui nigrum in candida vertunt,*
> *quis facile est aedem conducere, flumina, portus,*
> *siccandam eluviem, portandum ad busta cadaver,*
> *et praebere caput domina venale sub hasta.*
> *quondam hi cornicines et municipalis harenae*
> *perpetui comites notaeque per oppida buccae*
> *munera nunc edunt et, verso pollice vulgus*
> *cum iubet, occidunt populariter; inde reversi*
> *conducunt foricas, et cur non omnia? cum sint*
> *quales ex humili magna ad fastigia rerum*
> *extollit quotiens voluit Fortuna iocari.*

> I must say goodbye to my fatherland. Let Arturius and Catulus live there. Let the men who turn black into white stay on, men who find it easy to take on the contracts for temples, rivers, harbours, for draining floods and transporting corpses to the pyre – men who offer themselves for sale under the spear-sign of ownership. These former horn-players – the

permanent followers of country shows, their rounded cheeks a familiar
sight through all the towns – now stage gladiatorial shows themselves
and kill to please when the city mob demands it with a twist of the thumb.
From that they go back to their contracts for operating the public urinals
– and why draw the line at anything? After all, they're the type that
Fortune raises up from the gutter to a mighty height, whenever she
fancies a laugh. (Juvenal *Satires* III.29-40, tr. Braund)

This is quoted by a number of writers who state that it indicates that there
was a payment to use public latrines. However, the translation quoted
above gives us no reason to pursue this mythology.

The Price Edict of Diocletian (7.32) states that the pay for the *cloa-
carius*, the person who cleaned out the drains, was 25 *denarii* per day.

These various excerpts indicate that in Roman times there was an
awareness of aspects of life relating to lavatories and to the disposal of
urine and faeces both at a social/family level and also at the community
level. There exists a more subversive element of writing associated with
latrines and the people who used them, notably graffiti. What might we
learn from this about the lives of 'ordinary' people?

Graffiti survive from all parts of the Roman world. In Pompeii alone
1,500 have been recorded, scratched on the walls with a sharp instrument
or scrawled with charcoal or red chalk (Tanzer 1939: 3). All kinds of
subjects were covered, from election notices giving the names of the
candidates to announcements of gladiatorial shows. Food, wine and sex all
produced comments, often in or around work places such as bars or the
brothel at VII.12.18-20. One man, Aemilius Celer, has been identified as
the 'artist' associated with at least 35 graffiti (see Franklin 1991: n. 40).
There are six examples of alphabets scratched, perhaps by children, low
down on the walls.

Writing on latrine walls appears to have been as common then as it is
now. Obviously this indicates some degree of literacy. However, in the
Pompeiian graffiti a high percentage have spelling mistakes after the first
two or three words, which may lead us to assume that the people who
wrote most of them were not of the élite class. Both slaves and lower-class
freemen occupied places within a household which might necessitate being
able to spell and write to some degree.

Thousands of graffiti are included in the *Corpus Inscriptionum Latinarum*. One of the most philosophical, from Rome, translates as follows:
'Baths, wine and sex ruin our bodies, but what makes life worth living
except baths, wine and sex' (*CIL* VI.15258). In Pompeii graffiti abound,
among them 'Marcus loves Spendusa' (*CIL* IV.7086) and one in the atrium
of the House of Pinarius (VI.16.15) which can be translated as 'If anyone
does not believe in Venus they should gaze at my girl friend' (*CIL* IV.6842).
The writers are not all male: 'Cruel Lalagus, why do you not love me?' (*CIL*
3042). Perhaps if he had the inevitable might have occurred; outside the
Porta Nucera the result is recorded: 'Atimetus got me pregnant' (*CIL*

142

IV.10231). Although romance is commonplace, for example 'Celadus the Thracian [a famous gladiator] makes the girls sigh' (*CIL* IV.4397); sometimes the opposite is found: 'Serena hates Isidore' (*CIL* IV.3117). Occasionally there is a comment about someone's value: 'Litus, you are not worth an as' (*CIL* IV.10119). Perhaps inevitably this stretched to the price of prostitution. On the Via Sepulcrae Nuceriae can be found the following: 'Felix had it for one as' (*CIL* IV.5408). The situation could alter the value, to judge by this outside the Porta Marina: 'Let he who sits here think this above all things. If he wishes for sex Attica provides it for fifteen asses' (*CIL* IV.1751). Two graffiti in the basilica offer a salutary tale: 'O Chius I hope that your ulcerous pustules reopen and burn even more than they did before' (*CIL* IV.1820) and under it the following: 'Pyrrhus salutes his colleague Chius; I reluctantly heard of your death, and so, goodbye' (*CIL* IV.1852).

Graffiti associated with urination are less common than those relating to defecation. That somebody had a similar attitude to Juvenal (see p. 105) is demonstrated by an inscription on the forum arch at Thigibba in Tunisia which reads:

Si qui hic urinam fecerit, habebat Martem iratum

Anybody urinating here will incur the wrath of Mars (quoted in Wilson 2000)

In Pompeii there was a graffito to the left of the door of the House of Pascius Hermes which is virtually the same; only the god is different:

Cacator cave malum aut si contempseris habeas Iove iratum

To the one defecating here beware of the curse. If you scorn this curse you will have an angry Jupiter (*CIL* IV.7716)

By the Sepulcre of Caecilius Felix was the following.

Qui hic mixerit aut cacarit, habeat deos superos et inferos

May he who pisses or shits here incur the wrath of the gods above and below (*CIL* VI.13740, tr. Pascal)

Even more gods and goddesses were invoked at the Baths of Titus in Rome, with the following dire warning:

Duodecim deos et deanam et Iovem Optumum Maximu(m) habeat iratos quisquis hic mixerit aut cacarit

Twelve gods and goddesses and Jupiter, the biggest and best, will be angry with whoever urinates or defecates here (*CIL* VI.29848)

143

A simple statement was found in the House of the Gem in Herculaneum:

> *Appollinaris, medicus Titus Imp. hic cacavit bene*

> Appollinaris doctor of the Emperor Titus crapped well here (*CIL* IV.10619)

This was obviously written a very short time before the town was engulfed by hot mud, for Titus had become Emperor only a few weeks previously. The graffito was allegedly written by 'an irreverent servant' after the famous doctor had visited the house (Maiuri 1954: 64). Maiuri's guide book to Herculaneum neglects to print the word *cacavit*, due, no doubt, to the sensitivity of his readers.

In Pompeii can be found the almost identical messages *Cacator cave malum* (*CIL* IV.3782) and *Cave malum cacator* (*CIL* IV.4586): 'When you relieve yourself beware of evil.' As we have seen (above, p. 111) *Cacator cave malu(m)* was also found on a picture of a man between two serpents and the goddess Fortuna by the entrance to a latrine in Regio IX (*CIL* IV.3832). Pompeii contains other warnings about relieving oneself inappropriately. In Regio V was written:

> *Stercorari ad murum progredere si pre(n)sus fueris poena(m) patiare neces(s)e est, cave*

> If you shit against the walls and we catch you, you will be punished (*CIL* IV.7038)

A number of other warnings to those who defecate in the wrong place can be found from the Roman world. In Herculaneum this was written on a water tower:

> *(si qu)is velit in hunc locum stercus abicere monetur n(on) iacere siquis adver(sus ea) (n)idicium fecerit liberi dent (dena)rium n(on) servi verberibus in sedibus atmonentur.*

> Anyone who wants to defecate in this place is advised to move along. If you act contrary to this warning you will have to pay a penalty. Children must pay [number missing] denarii. Slaves will be beaten on their behinds. (*CIL* IV.10488)

A final warning for the slaves comes from Aquileia in the northern Adriatic.

> *Monentur domestici ne alibi quam in latrina cacent*

> Servants are to be reminded to shit in the latrine not elsewhere.

From Salona (a site 5 km from modern Split in Croatia) comes this graffito:

144

10. Who used these toilets?

*Quisquis in eo uico stercus non posuerit aut non cacauerit atque non
meiaurit habeat illas propitias. Si neglexerit, viderit.*

Whoever refrains from littering or pissing or shitting on this street may
the goddesses in general favour. If he does not do so let him watch out.
(*CIL* III.1966, tr. Pascal)

The wall opposite the latrine in the House of the Centenary (IX.8.3,6) in
Pompeii was covered with graffiti. One refers to Martha, presumably a
servant or slave.

Marthae hoc triclinium est, nam in triclinio cacat

This is Martha's triclinium: in fact she shits in the triclinium (*CIL*
IV.5243, tr. Pascal)

It seems that one graffito was not enough for some people; on the same
wall the following remark appears three times: 'Secundus defecated here'
(*CIL* IV.3146). It seems that somebody disliked someone in the house, for
on the same wall is written:

Quodam quisem testis eris quid senserim ubi cacatuiero veniam cacatum

Someday indeed you will learn how I feel. When you begin to shit I will
shit on you (*CIL* IV.5242, tr. Pascal)

Comments about defecation do not always appear within the confines of
the latrines. Just inside the Vesuvian Gate in Regio V is this one:

Cacator sic valeas, ut tu hoc locum transeas

Shit with comfort and good cheer, so long as you do not do it here (*CIL*
IV.6641)

This is obviously a warning, but is it purely to prevent a dirty mess or are
there overtones of religion or health? This appears on a wall in Regio II:

Lesbiane, cacas scribisque (sa)lute(m)

Lesbianus shits and writes 'Hello' (*CIL* IV suppl. 3.10070)

Martial shows that he and his readers are familiar with graffiti when
he tells Ligurra that she need not be afraid of him composing verses about
her – she isn't worth it.

*versus et breve vividumque carmen
in te ne faciam, times, Ligurra,*

et dignus cupis hoc metu videri.
sed frustra metuis cupisque frustra.
in tauros Lybici fremunt leones,
non sunt papilionibus molesti.
quaeras, censeo, si legi laboras,
nigri fornicis ebrium poetam,
qui carbone rudi putrique creta
scribit carmina, quae legunt cacantes.

You are afraid, Ligurra, of my writing verses against you, a brief lively poem, and you long to seem worthy of such an apprehension. But idle is your fear and idle your desire. Libyan lions roar at bulls, they do not trouble butterflies. I advise you, if you are anxious to be read of, to look for some boozy poet of the dark archway who writes verses with rough charcoal or crumbling chalk which folk read while they shit (Martial XII.61, tr. Shackleton Bailey)

The writings and graffiti quoted in this chapter take us back two thousand years, but it is only since the middle of the eighteenth century that scholars have been commenting on toilets. In the next chapter we will examine what they have said and place their comments in the context of their times.

11

Motions, maladies and medicine

My privy and well drain into each other
  After the custom of Christendie.
Fever and fluxes are wasting my mother.
  Why has the lord afflicted me?
                    Rudyard Kipling, *Natural Theology*

Were the Romans aware of the danger to public health that human effluent could pose? (see Koloski-Ostrow 2001: 98). Recently it has been suggested that any relatively structured society needs to deal with waste disposal in an expedient manner 'if it is to avoid a rapid escalation of infectious diseases' (Reimers 1991: 112). To relate this way of thinking to Roman times is to hazard conjectures about the thought processes of the people of that time and their knowledge of the causes of disease. Such interpretations may be far from the truth.

To arrive at a comprehensive understanding of the situation relating to the disposal of human excreta and its relevance to Roman culture we can look briefly at health and hygiene within the environment of a Roman city. Modern authors have been relatively unhelpful in discussing hygienic conditions, concentrating almost exclusively on water supplies (Amulree 1973; Scarborough 1980; Jackson 1988; Rosen 1993: 6-25). Urban drainage is often mentioned, but repetition of broad statements about latrines draining into sewers occurs (Isaac 1958: 10). Comparisons are frequently made with the conditions that existed in nineteenth-century London, but it is extremely difficult to arrive at a balanced judgement of hygienic standards in a place like Pompeii. Transmission of disease was ill understood, although Galen, writing almost a hundred years after the destruction of Pompeii, uses a 'seed' analogy as a hypothesis to explain contagion (see Nutton 1983).

There were many problems in maintaining health in Roman towns, not the least of which might have been associated with human excrement. Celsus comments:

> *Deiectionibus quoque si febris accessit, si inflammation iocineris aut prae-cordium aut ventris, si inmodica sitis, si longius tempus, si alvus varia, si cum dolore est, etiam periculum mortis subest, maximeque si inter haec tormina vera esse coeperunt; isque morbus maxime pueros absumit usque ad annum decimum: ceterae aetates facilius sustinent. Mulier quoque gravida eiusmodi casu rapi potest; atque, etiamsi ipsa convaluit, tamen*

partum perdit. Quin etiam tormina ab atra bile orsa mortifera sunt, aut si sub his extenuato iam corpore subito nigra alvus profluxit.

Again, in cases of diarrhoea, danger of death is at hand: if there is a fever in addition, if there is an inflammation of the liver or of the parts over the heart or of the stomach, if excessive thirst, if the affection is prolonged; if the stools are varied and passed with pain, and especially if with these signs true dysenteries set in; and this disease carries off mostly children up to the age of ten; other ages bear it more easily. Also a pregnant woman can be swept away by such an event, and even if she herself recovers, yet she loses the child. Dysenteries are fatal, moreover, when originated by black bile, or if a black motion suddenly issues from a body already wasted by dysentery. (Celsus *De Medicina* II.8.30-1, tr. Spencer)

A common nuisance resulting from the human and animal faecal waste, both in cesspits and in the streets, was the fly. Flies are not just irritating, they are potential carriers of disease. The Romans knew of some repellents, such as a mixture of coriander seed and olive oil, and sometimes a slave would fan off the flies.

Stat exoletus suggeritque ructanti
pinnas rubentes cuspidesque lentisci,
et aestuanti tenue ventilat frigus
supine prasino concubina flabello,
fugatque muscas myrtea puer virga.

[Dinner with Zoilus] A youth stands by, supplying red feathers and slips of mastic as he belches, while a concubine, lying on her back, makes a gentle breeze with a green fan to relieve his heat, and a boy keeps off the flies with a sprig of myrtle. (Martial III.82, tr. Shackleton Bailey)

This will have resulted in the flies being less of an inconvenience, but they will undoubtedly have settled on the food not only on the table but also in the kitchen, where in some cases the toilet was located.

Contaminated food transmits major diseases via the gastrointestinal tract. These may be broadly divided into three groups, caused by viral, bacterial and multicellular organisms. The bacterial diseases include cholera (*Vibrio cholerae*), food poisoning (*Salmonella* sp.) and Weil's disease (leptospirosis), and the multicellular include amoebic dysentery and helminthic infestation (intestinal worms) (Porter 1996: 378f.). In order to have some idea about the prevalence of these diseases it is necessary to have coprolite or tufa (see below, pp. 150, 153) to work on scientifically, and to have rigorous methodologies capable of identifying the organisms present while obviously bearing in mind the problems of contamination.

As we saw earlier, little is known about the washing of hands after using latrines in Roman times. Soap was unknown, although a case has been made for lomentum, a bean extract, being used as a cleansing agent

(Scarborough 1980: 39).There was no real understanding of 'germ theory', although in Varro's dissertation *On Agriculture* there is the following note.

Advertendum etiam, siqua erunt loca palustria, et propter easdem causas, et quod crescunt animalia quaedam minuta, quae non possunt oculi consequi, et per aera intus in corpus per os ac nares perveniunt atque efficiunt difficilis morbos.

Precautions must be taken in the neighbourhood of swamps, both for the reasons given, and because there are bred certain minute creatures which cannot be seen by the eyes, which float in the air and enter the body through the mouth and nose and there cause serious diseases. (Varro *On Agriculture* I.xii.2, tr. Hooper, revised Boyd Ash)

Celsus (*De Medicina* I.1.1-3) gives advice on how to maintain a healthy life style. His homily is addressed to educated upper-class readers in a financial position to take up his recommendations; it is most unlikely that a large proportion of the population would have been able to behave in the way he suggests. Most probably this period of history was not conducive to a healthy life; some statistics of life expectancy have been produced (though compiled from flawed data) which appear to confirm this (see Burn 1953; Hopkins 1966; Parkin 1992). If hygiene is recognised as 'public and private measures or actions taken to prevent diseases and to stay healthy' (Jansen 2000b: 275), then in Pompeii it is hard to find evidence for it.

Rome was plagued by malaria, which exacted a severe toll of life from young children, young mature adults and immigrants with no immunity. This disease 'readily coexists with gastro-intestinal infections such as typhoid, paratyphoid and amoebic dysentery' making them more danger-ous than in its absence (Scheidel 2003: 167). It cannot be said with any certainty that malaria was as great a problem in Pompeii. Indeed it is possible that the Bay of Naples, being a well documented retreat for the wealthy during the season in which the disease was at its most destruc-tive, was a relatively healthier area.

Work on materials from latrines with which archaeology is currently concerned shows a heightened awareness of the importance of new lines of scientific investigation. These may eventually lead to a greater under-standing of social conditions within Roman cities and allow us to make better comparisons of modern-day health with that of the people of first-century Pompeii.

We cannot, however, discuss toilets in Pompeii without commenting on modern research on the preserved 'faecal' material. From the middle of the twentieth century interest has increased in the information which may be obtained 'not only about the dietary preferences of groups and individuals but also about an individual's state of health, about techniques of food preparation, and about contemporary environmental conditions' (Bryant & Williams-Dean 1975: 100).

A couple of definitions may be helpful in the following discussion. (1) A *coprolite* is a recognisable faecal stool; this may be desiccated, mineralised or preserved in a water-based context (Holden 1991). (2) *Tufa* is the term applied to a calcareous deposit built up by the encapsulation of organic material due to the long-term action of minerals in water. A drain in the House of the Vestals contained highly mineralised organic material which was probably originally faecal material (Ciaraldi 2001: 66ff.). This is likely to have been the result of random refuse disposal rather than a regular occurrence. Similar evidence for human faeces has been found in drains in the Colonia at York (Hall & Kenward 1990: 391). Soil in archaeological deposits may, on biochemical analysis, be shown to have contents which indicate that faeces were deposited within that context (Bull et al. 2002).

The nature of faecal deposits in latrine pits is variable. In urban waterlogged sites, which give the best preservation (Greig 1982: 49), the fills may be black to olive green in colour and often sulphurous in odour, and there is good preservation of parasite ova and food residues (Jones 1992). The excavation of the Church Street Sewer in York was of a well-built drain with side channels entering it, in one of which (side passage 5) was found a deposit containing the larvae of *Psychodid* flies. These constitute a marker for faecal material. It was suggested that this was an additional use of the drain in the final phase of the system, its original purpose being to remove the waste water from the legionary bath house. Within the deposit were also found seeds of raspberry, elder and blackberry which perhaps were derived from human diet (Whitwell 1976: 24). It is obviously important to be certain that the material is of human origin. Coprolites of many herbivores such as deer, antelope, rabbits, cattle and horses can be easily recognised by their shape, size and predominantly grass and fibre contents. During chemical analysis in the laboratory there is a method for determining whether the coprolites are of human or non-human origin (Bryant 1974: 410).

There are no waterlogged deposits in Pompeii. However, it is possible to recover, from drains and cesspits, materials which have been thought to be associated with the disposal of human refuse. From these materials data can be obtained about intestinal parasites, pollen analysis, dietary residues and perhaps bacteria. The questions asked of these materials should throw light upon a number of aspects of Roman health, culture and behaviour.

In the excavation of VI.1 in Pompeii some mineralised material was recovered from a tile chute leading from the down pipe system into a cesspit. The laboratory analysis of this material showed *Trichuris* and *Ascaris* species ova (Dubbin 2003: 38). The presence of fly puparia casts as well as the parasites confirmed that the specimen was of faecal origin. The organic material in the specimen 'was preserved in a remarkable state, almost as if two thousand years had not passed' (Dubbin 2003: 35).Currently further specimens from down pipes are being examined and

Trichuris eggs have been found suggesting that parasitic infestation was common (Love 2007).

Bowel parasites have infested humans for many thousands of years. Little has been found by the way of intestinal parasites in Italian sites but the Romans were very familiar with a number of different types of worms.

> *Nonnumquam autem lumbrici quoque occupant alvum, hique modo ex inferioribus partibus, modo foedius ore redduntur; atque interdum latos eos, qui peiores sunt, interdum teretes videmus.*

> Again, worms also occasionally take possession of the bowel, and these are discharged at one time from the lower bowel, at another more nastily, from the mouth; and we observe them sometimes to be flattened [*Taenia solium*] which are the worst, or at times to be rounded [*Ascaris lumbricoides*]. (Celsus *De Medicina* IV.24, tr. Spencer)

The earliest report of the finding of parasite eggs from human body remains was made in 1910. Since then there have been a number of others. In Israel, parasite eggs and cysts of protozoan parasites (*Taenia* and *Trichuris*) were recovered from faecal residues (Cahill et al. 1991: 68), and long dried faecal samples from the Mesa Verde area revealed eggs of *Enterobius vermicularis* (Samuels 1965). Eggs of *Ascaris lumbricoides, Trichuris trichiura*, and *Dicrocoelium dendriticum* were found in the soil of a medieval pit in Winchester (Taylor 1955). The analysis of the material was more suggestive of porcine infestation than human, and later authors were also unsure whether the parasitic evidence discovered in another pit in the city was of human origin (Pike & Biddle 1966).

Pigs were kept in households in towns such as Winchester, Dorchester and Lincoln (Hall et al. 1983; Maltby 1994) and may have been part of similar arrangements in Pompeii. Quantitative analysis of *Trichurid* eggs in a number of different types of deposits showed that it was possible to identify primary faecal deposits with some certainty if the egg count was high (Jones 1985). Since then faecal material from Coppergate, York, containing *Ascaris* and *Trichuris* eggs has been described, indicating that at least part of the population suffered from heavy parasitic infestation (Kenward & Hall 1995). Eggs from *Trichuris* were discovered in the drain from the bath-house at Bearsden, Antonine Roman fort (Dickson 1979). In these last two cited publications was the suggestion that the mosses which were found in the sewage effluent might have been used as wiping material. Human faeces were shown to have formed part of the fill of a Roman well in the legionary fortress at York by the presence of ova of *T. trichuria* and *A. lumbricoides* (Kenward et al. 1986: 253). Analyses of three Roman cesspits from Causeway Lane, Leicester, showed that parasitic infection in the Roman world was widespread (Boyer 1999: 346). This was confirmed by the finding of eggs of whipworm, roundworm and tapeworm in the deposits of the latrine of a Roman centurion at Alphen aan den Rijn (Kuijper & Turner 1992).

What might the Romans have had in the way of treatment for all these parasites?

Si lati sunt, aqua potui dari debet, in qua lupinum aut cortex mori decoctus sit, aut cui adiectum sit contritum vel hysopum vel piperis acetabulum vel scamoniae paulum. Vel etiam pridie, cum multum alium ederit, vomat, posteroque die mali Punici tenues radiculas colligat, quantum manu comprehendet; eas contusas in aquae tribus sextariis decoquat, donec tertia pars supersit; huc adiciat nitri paulum, et ieiunus bibat. Interpositis deinde tribus horis duas potiones sumat, tum desidat subiecta calida aqua in pelve.

For the flat worms there should be given as draughts a decoction of lupins, or of mulberry bark, to which may be added, after pounding, either hyssop or a vinegar cupful of pepper, or a little scammony. Alternatively on one day let him eat a quantity of garlic and vomit, then on the next day take a handful of fine pomegranate roots, crush them and boil them in a litre and half of water down to one-third, to this add a little soda and drink it on an empty stomach. At three hours' interval let him take two further draughts, then, on going to stool, sit over a basin of hot water. (Celsus *De Medicina* IV.24, tr. Spencer)

Pollen grains which have been purposely or accidentally ingested pass through the alimentary tract virtually unaltered (Bryant & Williams-Dean 1975: 103) or as exines (Linskens & Jorde 1997: 83). In the first pollen analysis of human coprolites it was suggested that the ingested pollen contents of human faeces could provide information relating to the understanding of prehistoric diet, seasonal camp usage and medicinal use of certain plants (Martin & Sharrock 1964). Three medicinal species were posited when *Salix, Ephedra* and *Larrea* were found as high concentrations of pollen in coprolites from the south-western USA (Reinhard et al. 1991). Although the evidence is extremely circumstantial, the research thinking is highly appropriate to the identification of plants in Roman times, for which we have extremely good evidence of pharmaceutical usage from writers such as Dioscorides. Pollen analysis from ancient cesspits in Jerusalem showed four different plant families, mustard, carrot, mint and daisy (Cahill et al. 1991). It was surmised that although these could have had medicinal qualities, they may have indicated a restricted diet during the siege of the city by Nebuchadnezzar in 586 BCE. Pollen analysis in urban contexts is challenging for a number of reasons, not least the difficulty of knowing its exact place of origin. Some research has been carried out on pollen from soil samples from the 79 CE levels in Pompeii, Oplontis and Boscoreale, but pollen survival is poor because of microbiological decomposition. The evidence is limited due to the difficulty of identification beyond the family level. The samples also give a distortion of the botanical range because some plants were not allowed to flower (Dimbleby 2002: 181f.; Grüger 2002: 211).

Given the right conditions for preservation it is possible to identify dietary residues in faecal material. Almost a hundred years ago sunflower seeds, water-melon seeds and fragments of hickory shell were found in coprolites from Salts Cave, Kentucky (Young 1910). Fifty years later detailed microscopic examination of human coprolite from a Peruvian midden dated around 3000 BCE gave information about the diet of the person who had excreted the faecal material (Callen & Cameron 1960). A dietary chronology over a period of nearly 8,000 years was established from coprolites from Tamaulipas, Mexico (Callen 1969). Further work on diet, as demonstrated by the analysis of desiccated coprolites from northern Chile, has given a good insight into prehistoric human subsistence in the area and showed a strong emphasis on the exploitation of Andean camelids as well as wild vegetable resources (Holden 1991). Among the many reports from the Americas was the analysis of eight desiccated human palaeofaeces which gave evidence of diet, *Iva annua, Chenopodium berlandieri* and *Helianthus annuus* as well as endoparasitic infection with *Ascaris lumbricoides, Giardia intestinalis*, and possibly a member of the *Ancylostomoidea* (Faulkner 1991).

In the material from the latrine at Alphen aan den Rijn, several cereals were identified including oil seeds, spices, fruit and nuts. Among these were species imported from the Mediterranean region, such as aniseed, celery, coriander, caraway, fennel, grape, olive, peach, chestnut, walnut and fig. In addition there was evidence of freshwater fish and seafood such as oysters and mussels (Kuijper & Turner 1992).

A review of the analysis of latrine and drain residues in various areas of the Roman Empire shows that not only can information be procured about the diet but also, indirectly, the movement of exotic goods over large distances can be demonstrated (Dickson & Dickson 2000). That this process occurred over a period of time with new species being introduced is shown in the analysis of material from three Roman, nine medieval and three early modern cesspits in the Lower Rhineland (Knörzer 1984).

It is important to be aware of the circumstances in sites like Pompeii that may lend themselves to the preservation of this type of material and to search diligently in the areas where it may be found. Organic material in cesspits is usually well preserved when there is a high moisture content, but in badly drained contexts mineralisation can also give good conservation. The most resistant parts of the food are chaff, rachis fragments, fruit and weed seeds, and bone fragments.

A most interesting recent publication on the scanning electron microscopy of a single carbonised cheese found in Herculaneum recorded the presence of *cocci* identified as *Brucella melitensis* bacteria (Capasso 2002). This appears to corroborate the osteological pattern of brucellosis bone lesions which was identified in the skeletons at Herculaneum

(Capasso 2000). However, the bacteriological identification of the organisms of *Brucella melitensis* is purely morphological, and although it is possible that the *cocci* are as supposed there cannot be any certainty (Dr D. Birkenhead, Consultant Microbiologist, Huddersfield Royal Infirmary: personal communication). DNA studies may produce a more certain result.

12

Who cares about latrines?

Many early authors who wrote about Pompeii were particularly concerned with the forum, the tombs, the theatres and so on and had little interest in toilets – even when they were describing the houses (e.g. Breton 1855, De Jorio 1828, Horne 1895). 'Beginning with the standard works by Overbeck and Mau, most published studies treat Pompeii topographically … As a result, virtually no attempts have been made to acquire an overview of the whole city and to distinguish the various historical layers in its fabric' (Zanker 1998: 30). This comment applies especially to the study of latrines.

An exception to this was Gusman, who at least provided a drawing of a latrine (Fig. 138), but unfortunately he neither gives us its location nor expands upon it in any way (Gusman *c.* 1900: 282). In his *Scatological Rites* Bourke comments 'In ancient Rome there were public latrines but no privies attached to houses' (Bourke 1891: 135). This is in direct contrast to the comments of Lanciani who, when he writes about domestic toilets in Rome, states that he has excavated hundreds, none of which communicate with the drains under the streets (Lanciani 1873).

It is possible that there was a deliberate avoidance of discussion of this topic. For example, the large public toilet in the forum is not shown on the

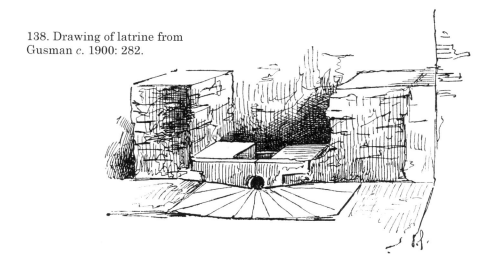

138. Drawing of latrine from Gusman *c.* 1900: 282.

plan in the first major book on Pompeii written in English (Gell & Gandy 1852: between pp. 150 & 151). Another author identifies it as a prison (Breton 1855, after p. 372). This may reflect the prudish nature of society at the time, or it may continue a previous author's misidentification, since Dyer also shows it as a prison (Dyer 1867), as does the map in vol. I of *Pompeii* published by the Library of Entertaining Knowledge (Clarke 1831) (see Fig. 139).

The most descriptive entry on the subject of the 'latrina' during the late nineteenth century is to be found in the *Dictionnaire des antiquités grecques et romaines* (Daremberg & Saglio 1873-1910: 987-91). In addition to a general discussion of latrines in the Greek and Roman periods, it deals in some depth, and with a high degree of accuracy, with the situation in Pompeii, commenting that 'without exception every house in Pompeii has a latrine', and describing their situations: 'The custom of placing the latrine in the kitchen is far from being the general rule.' 'Often the latrine is to be found in the depths of the house, or else opening onto the hallway or using spare space under the staircase.' It also mentions those of the upper storeys: 'On the first storey there were latrines which connected by a pipe with those of the ground floor or were provided with their individual waste pipe.' Much of this entry on latrines, which was written by Henry Thédenat, has been confirmed by examination of latrines throughout the city and in particular the illustration in the *Dictionnaire* of the latrine and a down pipe (Fig. 140) is easily recognisable as the one in VII.9.63 discussed earlier (p. 69).

The recording of the city by Fiorelli indicates that he was fully aware of the latrines within the city, mentioning among others those in VI.1.1; VI.1.2; VI.1.9-10; VI.1.12; VI.1.13; VI.1.17 and VI.1.18 (Fiorelli 1875).

In 1900 the excavation of four latrines by Sogliano was recorded in the *Notizie Scavi* (Sogliano 1900). These all drained into cesspits of varying depths and constructions. They were as follows. The first at VI.10.14 was 11.2 m deep with a circular diameter of 1 m. The one at VII.14.25, of rectangular construction 1.5 m x 2.2 m, was 6.3 m deep. The third in a shop, VII.12.11, was an ellipse with the greatest axis of 1.5 m and smallest 0.95 m and a greatest depth of 5.40 m. Finally the fourth latrine, at VII.7.10, resembled a cistern, lined with plaster, with a mouth 0.60 m in diameter and a bell-shaped expansion below the ground to a depth of 5.3 m. This 'cesspit' also had a branch at the bottom turning south towards the Via Marina. The contents of three of these cesspits were of 'volcanic debris' (is this a reference to *lapilli*?) and only in VII.14.25 was there discovered 'one dark coloured stratum from whence came a nauseating smell!'.

Ten years after Sogliano's publication, Thédenat discussed latrines and their positioning within the Pompeian dwelling. He noted their initial proximity to the cooking area and also that, over a period of time, they were moved to other parts of the dwelling and to the upper storey. He commented that rarely were the latrines connected to sewers, but unfor-

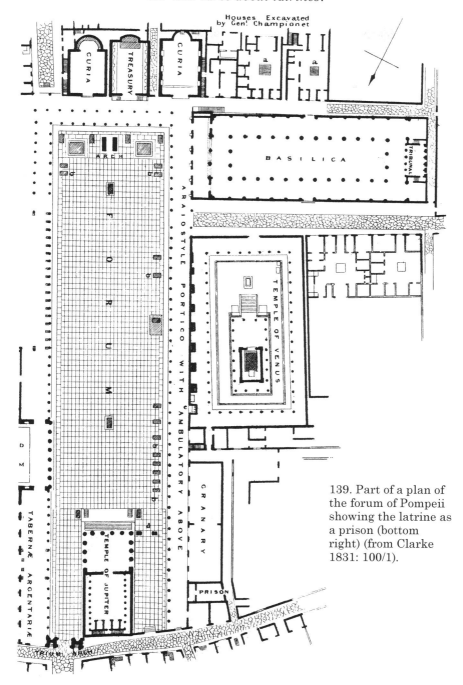

139. Part of a plan of the forum of Pompeii showing the latrine as a prison (bottom right) (from Clarke 1831: 100/1).

140. Drawing of down pipe
with latrine (from
Daremberg & Saglio
1873-1910).

tunately gave no examples. He did, however, give five examples in which
latrines emptied directly onto the road or sidewalk (II.4.41; III.7.1; IV.3.24;
IV.7.10; VI.15.5) (Thédenat 1910: 96). Each of these addresses has been
checked and no evidence has been found of latrines emptying directly onto
the sidewalk. Perhaps Thédenat was implying drainage of latrines into
cesspits in the sidewalks. These occur all over the city of Pompeii, not just
as described in VI.1. However, there is no evidence of these features either,
although they could be lying, invisible, beneath modern surfaces.

That some professions had a degree of curiosity about latrines is indicated by a paper in the Proceedings of the Royal Society of Medicine
concerning the multi-seat latrine in Dougga in Tunisia. Although a surgeon, not an archaeologist, the author measured the distances between the
seats (23 in/ 58 cm) and the diameter of the apertures (6 in/ 15 cm), and
also made interesting comments about the drainage and the water supply
(Berry 1921). It is early work of this nature that has stimulated later
authors to estimate the seating capacity of house toilets.

Much early writing related to water systems, and comments about
refuse disposal were supported by little or no evidence. Perhaps there was
an assumption from the ancient literature (see Strabo *Geography* V.3.8)
and from the finding of what are referred to as 'sewers' or *cloacae*, that

there was a system connecting water drainage and sewage disposal throughout Roman towns, and therefore in Pompeii. This belief was by no means universal. As we saw on p. 130, Mau, writing at the end of the nineteenth century, produced a somewhat more accurate interpretation: 'There were covered conduits to carry off the surface water of the forum, one of which runs under the Strada delle Scuole to the south, the other under the Via Marina to the west. Elsewhere the water rushed down the streets till it came near the city walls, where it was collected and carried off by large storm sewers. One is at the west end of the Vico dei Soprastanti, another at the west end of Nola Street, and a third leads from Abbondanza Street, where it is crossed by Stabian Street, toward the south.' He went on to say that 'there were other sewers in the city, but they were of small dimensions and had not been fully investigated. In general they seem to have been under sidewalks. They were not designed to receive surface water, but the drainage of houses. They cannot have served this purpose fully, however, for *most of the closets were connected, not with the sewers, but with cesspools* [my italics] (Mau 1902: 229). Despite this, late into the twentieth century an author could comment as follows: 'The overflow water (from cisterns) ran out onto the roadway and this was also true of waste water, including that of latrines' (Adam 1994: 261). It has since been demonstrated that, as far as the latrines of VI.1 are concerned, this was not the case. Interest in the planning of ancient towns brought comparisons of systems of drainage in Aosta, Timgad, Emona and Lincoln (Haverfield 1913). In all cases the drains are referred to as sewers. However, there is no scrupulous definition of the function of the system, and it is easy to assume, wrongly, that human waste was poured into these drains.

Early in the twentieth century a work by Mygind was published, entitled *Hygienische verhaltnisse im alten Pompeji* (1921). This was described in 1986 as being 'by far the most comprehensive study of all aspects of hygiene at Pompeii'. Among other details about latrines and drainage systems dealt with in this work, the author describes the various situations within the properties in which latrines are found – noting that each house had its own, even the smallest dwelling. This, he said, also applied to many shops, workshops and most drinking establishments. Some houses had two latrines on the ground floor, and he suggests that some latrines were two-seaters (IX.iii.31) or even three-seaters (IX.ii.27). Latrines, he states, were usually sited somewhere secluded in the house. If they were in a separate room it was usually a very small one without a door and possibly with a curtain across the opening. If the latrine was in the kitchen area there was sometimes a chest-high wall separating it from the cooking surface. He believes that ash was used to cover excrement in the cesspit to reduce smell, or perhaps to create garden fertiliser. Some kitchens had window openings and holes in the ceiling to allow fumes to escape.

He affirms that no waste pipes from toilets open into the street and observes that there were latrines on the first floor with visible pipes down to cesspits, giving as examples I.1.8; VII.2.20; I.2.7 and VIII.4.4. He describes sloping platforms making it easy to keep the toilets clean and suggests that they could have been used for the disposal of waste water.

Perhaps mistakenly, he surmises that the seats were probably made of stone and often just rested on plinths because the slot was much too wide for even the heaviest wooden plank. He notes that a stone seat was found at IX.5.9 but 'is no longer there'. He also comments that all the public toilets emptied into sewers whereas only a few latrines in private houses did so. He thinks that the graffiti indicate that people defiled the streets and public places with faeces. Interestingly, he states that latrines were used by family members, slaves and clients but then goes on to say that the upper classes used chamber pots or portable commodes.

Mygind's work, though it was published over eighty years ago, still stands out as a masterpiece. It has never been translated into English, which is a great loss to those modern students who do not read German.

A much less thorough account of the history of drainage, irrigation, sewage disposal and water supply was written in 1929 (Garrison 1929). A brief paragraph informs us that 'water closets of modern pattern have been excavated at Babylon, Nineveh, Knossos, Tel-el-Amarna [1400 BCE], Cairo [640 BCE], Priene and Pompeii'. However, the author leaves the subject of latrines and sewage disposal in the Roman world to concentrate on water supply and drainage systems.

Within academic circles there appears to have been little interest in the subject for the forty years that followed the 1920s. In 1960 the production of an exhibition feature at Olympia stimulated the publication of a history of bathrooms and toilets. This was intended for general interest and was hugely informative but unfortunately poorly referenced (Wright 1960).

A chance find of a Roman toilet seat at Neatham (Redknap 1976a) stimulated an undergraduate dissertation on Roman latrines and urban sanitation (Redknap 1976b). The classical background to the work was particularly thorough and covered a wide-ranging set of subjects, from latrines and chamber pots (which he noted are referred to in Latin as *matellae, scaphii, matulae* or *matellii*) to problems of sanitation and disease. His few references to Pompeii include 'the latrine in the south east corner of the Bar of Phoebus' (VI.1.19). This feature is now considered to be a cistern, the latrine being a matter of only 3 m away in another small room (Hobson 2004).

Stone toilet seats have been found overlying cesspits in the old City of David (Jerusalem) dating to the seventh to sixth centuries BCE, indicating that this technology was widespread in the first millennium BCE (Cahill et al. 1991). It is this historical approach and the questions which it raises about the development of 'latrine technology' that gives depth to our understanding of the situation in Pompeii.

Unfortunately little more came of the subject of latrines until the publication of a wide-reaching article on 'Slums, sanitation and mortality in the ancient world' (Scobie 1986). Linking the sanitation of Roman cities to perceptions of life expectancy and mortality in the Roman Empire, this broadened the whole perspective by exploring the physical aspects of latrines and effluent disposal. Within this work, areas for research were identified which subsequent workers have devoted much of their time to exploring. The work has been expanded on by Andrew Wilson, who has given an extremely succinct, historical and descriptive analysis of drainage and sanitation systems in the ancient world (Wilson 2000). After citing the earliest known comprehensive network at Mohenjo-Daro with its latrines with vertical chutes into drains or cesspits in the streets, he points out that centuries later, in the Roman period, there was considerable variation in the effectiveness of drainage systems in cities of the western world and quotes Strabo on the filth covering the streets of Smyrna.

In the last decade of the twentieth century most of the new work on Roman toilets has been done by Gemma Jansen (Jansen 1993, 1994, 1997, 2000, 2001), with some by Koloski-Ostrow (Koloski-Ostrow 2000, 2001) and de Haan (de Haan 2001). Jansen's analysis of paintings in Roman toilets (Jansen 1993) is instrumental in indicating the social distinctions that occurred within the confines of what, in many houses, was a small, dark and smelly room, although the comment that only a dozen latrines are still decorated gives a somewhat false impression (that many of the rooms were plastered can still be seen throughout Pompeii).

These recent studies on latrines and their drainage systems have been based on the 79 CE levels in Pompeii, and as a result suffer from two major problems. First, they discuss only the city as it was at that point, making no allowances for changes over time. The establishment of typologies of latrines based on their construction, and suggesting advances in technology without a full understanding of the changes which may or may not have occurred over time, make interpretations from this type of data extremely tenuous. Secondly, the numbers of toilets identified have clearly visible remains. The excavations in VI.1 have shown that there were and are many more that are present but not obvious. Also a number of toilets have been destroyed or built over in the course of providing modern facilities within the ancient city (Jansen 1997: 122 n. 4).

The magnificent series of descriptions of Pompeian houses, *Häuser in Pompeji*, has followed on this analysis of the 79 CE levels. The latrines within the houses are defined and described but each one is taken as a separate entity. In Ling's excellent analysis of the standing monument of the *insula* of the Menander, he points out that there were latrines in all of the houses in I.10 at the time of the eruption. In mentioning that one latrine (in I.10.10,11) was a late addition to that house, he does give a small degree of diachronicity to the work (Ling 1997: 209). However, only the results of the excavation of a whole *insula*, such as that undertaken by the Anglo-American Project in Pompeii, can show how important it is to describe how changes over time have influenced the visible 79 CE levels.

In particular, it has shown that latrines may be taken out of use in one part of the 'house' to allow for changes in the use of space, while the necessary facility is provided in a different area of the building. An isolated example of research along these lines was the study of the latrines in one *insula* in Ostia of the mid-fourth century CE (Boersma 1996). Here the author states that 'the presence or absence of a latrine in a domestic building is one of the instruments to gain insight into the social standards of a building and the status of the people who lived and worked in it'.

Very little research has gone into analyses of the contents of cesspits or latrines. There appears in some cases to have been a total disregard for the information which might be obtained from the materials within the collection conduits of latrines. An example of this is at the toilet in the Via Garibaldi, Rome, where for many years emphasis on the preservation of the plaster and its paintings took precedence over any other research. The small allocation of work allowed for 'the cleaning of the channel for foul water' was carried out without an analysis of the contents (Chini 1995).

Occasionally a latrine has been excavated and a comment made about its contents. 'In the kitchen (of the House of the Coloured Capitals) it soon became clear that the southern part had never been completely excavated. It is occupied by a latrine which yielded a large number of pottery fragments, all of which appear to date pre-62 CE' (Descoeudres & Sear 1987).

The excavation of the latrine in the House of the Tragic Poet appears to confirm the use of water regularly to flush out the contents, leaving it empty (Wood 1996: 36). However, it is likely that Sogliano's excavations indicate that natural degradation over 2,000 years leaves little material lying in the cesspits.

The collection of urine for industrial purposes has already been commented upon. At Selinus, where the toilet space adjoined the bathroom, it has been suggested that the drain to the street outside was flushed with the dirty bath water. As a corollary to this it was surmised that urine alone went down this drain, and that faecal excrement was collected in chamber pots and disposed of as fertiliser (Crouch 1993: 303).

In the baths of Mithras at Ostia the urine from a urinal was said to have been collected into 'an amphora' for use in *fullonicae* in the basement (Crouch 1993: 303), although this is questioned by Miko Flohr in a forthcoming publication (Flohr, personal communication).

Finally, there has been little or no comment upon the siting of latrines in the upper storeys of buildings, and the social significance of such a change. In a study entitled *Upstairs at Pompeii* the types of space which the upper storeys may have provided is explored (Young 1997: 10). However, although living space is discussed, the provision of latrines, which would have been an additional 'luxury', is not mentioned. Other suggestions for the use of upper storey space, such as storage, would not have introduced the need to move the latrines from the ground floor. As previously discussed, the existence of down pipes can be noted throughout

Pompeii, with some *insulae* having many and some none at all – indicating the degree of utilisation of upper storeys for living accommodation, and changes in social stratification over time. More work needs to be done on this subject to parallel the way in which modern research is extending our knowledge of diet and disease.

13

Future research?

We saw earlier that latrine systems pre-dated Roman times. A terracotta latrine from Olynthus pre-dates Pompeii by several hundred years (Crouch 1993: 249).

The historical continuity of latrines within the different *insulae* in Regio VI at Pompeii confirms the movement of toilet facilities away from kitchens to small rooms adjacent to entrances with access to the streets for cesspit disposal of the effluent and later to upper storey latrines.

Most of the latrine construction technology is of mixed stone and mortar. However, in one case (VI.5.4) brick construction, probably of the first century CE, is identifiable. The lack of preservation of wood has meant that seat material and design is hypothetical, resulting in discussion about a few latrines which might have seated more than one person. However, plaster marks and slots in the masonry of the walls are good indicators for height and size of the seating.

Jansen attempts to describe a typology of latrines (Jansen 1997: 124f.). She represents these by two diagrams. The first she calls a 'flush toilet' and the second a 'niche toilet' (Figs 141 & 142). This classification lacks

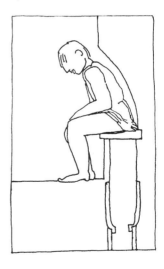

141. Flush toilet (from Jansen 1997: 124).

142. Niche toilet (from Jansen 1997: 125).

165

some clarity as it is likely that all latrines in Pompeii were flushed with water to some extent. The data from excavation and survey of Regiones VI and VII enable us to recognise the structural content within this typology, but it leads to a degree of confusion because it assumes that water was not used for the niche type. Indeed Jansen emphasises this difference when she states in her doctoral thesis that there is no need to flush the niche type because the user is directly above the drain (Jansen 1997: 124f.). However, it seems completely unrealistic to suppose that an upstairs niche toilet would not have been flushed: its down pipe might easily become blocked, especially during the warm summer season. There does not appear to be a straightforward reason for the existence of the two types of lavatory Jansen describes. Both types occur in VI.1 and are common throughout the city. There is no evidence in VI.1 for one type being superseded by the other except on a chronological basis, in the case of those on upper storeys. It appears likely that property owners chose the type of toilet on a purely pragmatic basis, perhaps depending upon available space, especially with those that appear to be late additions. Social and financial elevation in the first century CE, as seen in the massive reorganisation in the House of the Vestals, was not unusual. In this house this development appears to have isolated the latrine from the more opulent rooms of the house, especially the peristyle area. This may indicate a change in use by the élite of the house, who probably resorted to the use of chamber pots to be emptied by servants. This was a different situation from the busy business world of the Via Consolare where there was a high demand for latrine facilities, probably mainly for male customers, though the degree of privacy offered would not preclude female usage. The late addition of a toilet in the Bar of Acisculus suggests a response to a demand.

The archaeological evidence on the positioning of cesspits has thrown some light on a number of questions. Jansen has suggested that these were positioned outside houses so that 'the pit could be emptied without causing a mess in the house' (Jansen 2000: 38). In addition, and somewhat contrarily, she also suggests that the cesspits in Pompeii would not require emptying because liquids could permeate 'through the seams between the bricks' (Jansen 2000: 38). There are undoubtedly other reasons for having cesspits in the 'open air' of the street (though they almost certainly had covers of wood or stone). These include the physical (e.g. the obnoxious smell), cultural (e.g. attitudes to excreta), and chemical (e.g. the production of methane from the waste). This latter product might have provided a known danger to anyone using the facility while holding a naked flame in a lamp, but surprisingly we do not appear to have any reference to explosions in latrines. What about those latrines whose cesspits were not outside in the street? Would the House of the Vestals toilet with its cesspit have been in an open room with no roof? It might have been unpleasant to use the facility if it was completely open to the elements, as the weather in Pompeii can be quite cold and wet. However, with the sloping tile flooring the rain would act as a cleanser and there might be less smell and danger. Anyway, there is sufficient evidence to suggest that most toilets were in enclosed areas with ceilings.

No single method of dating that applies directly to latrines has been established. Occasionally artefacts are found that indicate an event in the chronological sequence, as with the contents of the cesspit on the ramp leading up to the House of the Triclinium (VI.1.1) (see p. 97). However, other aspects of the archaeology have provided an answer to the question which latrines were in use in 79 CE and which were not? The phasing of the *insula* indicates that there were late additions, including the system in VI.1.1 when the House of the Triclinium was constructed (*c.* 20 CE) and also the latrine in the Bar of Acisculus. This suggests that provisions were being made for toilet facilities in what appears to have been a very active social area of the city. Modifications in the mosaic phase of the House of the Vestals, with the closure of the toilet and change of use of a kitchen room at the east of the house, were consistent with some areas of the house being upgraded and others being designated service areas. The addition of upper storeys to the buildings in the *insula* also allowed for toilets to be moved into the new living quarters accessed by the various staircases.

Throughout these changes the technology for the collection and disposal of refuse in the city of Pompeii did not appear to change. The reason for this is the use of deep cesspits which, allowing for proper care and attention with frequent water flushing, was a proven and successful method that required little other management. However, some particular circumstances did allow for drains and sewers to be combined.

Urban drainage systems can be classified into four categories. First-order refers to water drains such as gutter spouts from roofs or channels from latrines or baths. A combination of several of these channels in one building produces a second-order drain which, combined with similar systems from other buildings, forms the third category of drains under the streets. These may finally flow into large collectors, fourth-order drains, which eventually discharge outside the settlement (Wilson 2000: 152). All the systems in VI.1 fall neatly into the first and second orders. There is some collateral drainage of excrement along with water from the main city baths, as has been noted. This conforms to the third and fourth orders (Wilson 2000:152).

The paving of the streets of Pompeii, which was carried out around the start of the imperial Roman period, would have provided an opportunity for sewers to be dug, to which cesspit drainage could have been attached (cf. development in Herculaneum in Jansen 2000: 43). That this was not done might suggest that the system operating at that time worked sufficiently well for it not to be altered, although to drain the whole of the city would have involved considerable expense for no perceived benefit to the élite.

As previously noted, there are terracotta pipes, often inserted into walls, running downwards from either upper storeys or roofs. Although these have been commented on for over a hundred years, little or no work has been carried out on their implications. Mygind comments on the use of vertical pipes in external house walls from the upper storey for removal of waste water, and notes that in some cases there were pipes connecting a latrine (upper storey) to a cesspit (Mygind 1921: 269f.). Packer comments that in the *stabulum* I.1.6-9, there is a latrine on the ground floor and that 'the second floor also had a latrine above this room' (Packer 1978: 9). Presumably he draws this conclusion from a down pipe. The distribution of down pipes in the remainder of Regio VI suggests that some of the *insulae* had more upper storey residential accommodation than others (VI.3 compared with VI.9).

As was discussed in Chapter 6, a number of latrines in private properties accommodated more than one person, but it appears likely that over two or more centuries there was a cultural shift towards single-seaters. The few remaining latrines for more than one person were almost exclusively in the working quarters of the slaves/servants.

In his 'Inns at Pompeii' Packer shows a number of different types of inns, restaurants and bars (Packer 1978: 11, 17, 35). Only one of these, at I.2.24, has its latrine as part of the kitchen. The siting of the latrines in other examples is most often 'off a narrow corridor' (e.g. VII.12.34; VII.12.35; V.2.13). In all of these there would have been a good deal of privacy. Another latrine, V.2.13, is described as being at the end of a narrow corridor containing a staircase 'separated from room 2 by a now vanished partition'. This observation is confirmed by the survey of Regio VI.

In modern western societies privacy norms are cultural and vary with socio-economic status and family values. Crowded living conditions force upon people a lack of privacy. Institutional behaviours, which are highly structured and authoritarian, reinforce the relative unimportance and anonymity of the individual (Kira 1970). Changes in Roman culture may have contributed to the fact that latrine systems appear to have been moved away from the kitchen/latrine milieu to more secluded areas, such as under staircases, or into specially adapted small rooms (and also to upper storeys, where unfortunately little is known of the extent of privacy). This would suggest that, using the one characteristic of 'direct visibility' of the toilet, there is evidence that 'not seen' comes into consideration as a matter of privacy. Seneca's comment about the German gladiator being allowed solitude at the latrine also suggests 'not seen'. Although there are no surviving doors to toilet rooms, there are many marks in threshold stones to suggest that such existed. If doors were absent there may have been curtains, or wooden screens, to decrease direct visual contact.

One of the questions to be asked about the social aspects of latrines is who used them and how accessible they were. Descriptions of the latrines associated with the bars in VI.1 make it obvious that these were provided as a facility for customers. Were they also available to passers-by or were there other options? A room entered directly off the Via Abbondanza, VII.14.4, is a case in point. Here is a small room with only one entrance from which it is likely that there was an access staircase to the upper storey. At the rear of the room is a latrine, sheltered slightly from the view of people in the street. Was this for public use, or was there a locked doorway giving access only to those people with keys (who perhaps inhabited the rooms upstairs)?

Room size, lighting and decoration are important factors for consideration. A number of the latrines in *insulae* 2-16, which were situated by outside walls, had windows. An assumption is made that most if not all of the rooms housing latrines would have been dark and that light would have been provided by a lamp, sometimes housed in a niche in the wall (Mygind 1921: 319). There is very little evidence for this in any of the latrines in Pompeii although coincidentally a lamp was found in the excavation of AA185, perhaps dropped accidentally into the latrine. A small number of the latrines surveyed in Regio VI were in rooms which are very gloomy (VI.7.20,21,22; VI.9.6; VI.12; VI.15.8,9). In addition there are some latrines in extremely dark underground cellars.

The latrine in the House of the Vestals is positioned in the work area, described as the locus for the dirty or polluted activities of the house (Hales 2003). This positioning appears to be repeated in other high-class dwellings such as the House of the Small Fountain, House of the Bear, House of the Grand Duke and House of the Ceii. There is an argument that this area would not have been used by members of the élite family. Generalisations of this type have to take into account the positioning of latrines in other grand houses. Thus in the House of the Golden Cupids and the House of Paquius Proculus the latrines are directly off the peristyle, which was an area certainly used by the élite. Mygind comments that only a small number of latrines have wall decoration, finding only three latrines with highly decorated walls (Mygind 1921: 319). Jansen describes a dozen such in Pompeii and Herculaneum and concludes that the decoration is functional; she identifies the latrine as being part of the service and working space of the house (Jansen 1993). It would be a waste of money for the élite to decorate parts of the house that they did not frequent. Allowing for the deterioration of the properties which has occurred over the last two hundred years, most of the latrines in Regiones VI and VII can be shown to have been plastered. The quality of the decoration is, unfortunately, unknown.

The evidence of direct refuse disposal in latrines is hardly overwhelming. One latrine, the one in the House of the Vestals, has a drain from another room emptying directly into the cesspit. Nor has the excavation material obtained from the cesspits been helpful in attempting to pursue this question, because in most cases *lapilli* have been the most common findings. The one cesspit in which a large amount of Roman waste material was discovered may be an anachronism.

Logically those latrines in close proximity to kitchens might have been used to dispose of waste from that area. However, many of the latrines in Regio VI are well away from kitchens, and other methods of clearance of rubbish must be taken into account.

It is also less than satisfying to admit that there are huge gaps in our knowledge of aspects of health and hygiene in the Roman world. That there was a complete lack of understanding of the hazards to health involved in the disposal of human excrement in Pompeii is obvious. The steps that were taken to flush their latrines were almost certainly concerned with smell, perhaps with some degree of personal cleanliness, and possibly with some sort of understanding that water helped in the natural decomposition of the cesspit material.

In the examination of the latrine pit soils of Jerusalem the remains of faecal matter were found to be mixed with calcareous ash which was believed to have been introduced 'to sanitise the contents of the latrine by reducing bacterial and fungal activity' (Cahill et al. 1991: 67). This is an extraordinarily speculative statement. Even to state confidently that it reduced the smell would require suitable experimental work. As we have seen, assumptions should not be made on the basis of current knowledge. Koloski-Ostrow attempts to clarify the position by quoting six modern criteria for public health protection in the disposal of human waste (Koloski-Ostrow 1996: 83f.). It is probable that only one of these, that which refers to nuisance due to odour or unsightly appearance, would have elicited any sort of response from a Pompeian in the first century CE. Nevertheless, an attempt must be made to understand the cultural controls which governed the disposal of human waste at the time.

Structural and contextual bases for the study of Roman latrines have now been well established. The following areas can be identified as potential avenues for further research.

It would be extremely valuable to excavate more latrine systems in Pompeii, with special attention to fills. To obtain the most information, it would be best if a system of safe deep excavation were available. Coring is unlikely to give a totally satisfactory result since large artefacts would be missed. However, it is possible that there is identifiable waste material preserved at the bottom of the deep cesspits. Health and safety factors may render this aspect of archaeological research impracticable. Recently the Soprintendenza of Pompeii has ruled against excavation deeper than 2 m without shoring.

More research into upper storeys is required to establish the presence of the latrines, and to further investigate the contents of down pipes. In a sealed situation there may be material adhering to the linings of the pipes which would repay laboratory evaluation. This might be extended by the identification of faecal deposits in contexts such as drains by means of biomarkers (see Bull et al. 2002). At present this type of work has some problems with species specificity, but these might be overcome by contextual analysis.

Much remains to be discovered about Roman latrines. Perhaps the contents of this book will give impetus to scholars in the future to increase our understanding of a basic behaviour, the disposal of human waste in the Roman world.

Glossary

atrium: the 'central' area of the house from which access was gained to rooms and corridors.

caldarium: the hot room of a bath house.

castellum [a small castle]: in Pompeii the name given to the building which received the water from the aqueduct and distributed it through three channels into the piped system for the city.

caupona: a bar.

cesspit: '(1) a pit for the reception of night-soil and refuse, a midden; (2) a well sunk to receive the soil from a water closet, kitchen sink, etc.: properly one which retains the solid matter and allows the liquid to escape' (*OED* 1970).

cocciopesto (*opus signinum*): a common flooring made of mortar with large amounts of crushed tile, brick or marble fragments.

compluvium: the opening in the roof above the atrium which allowed in light and also rainwater which fell into the *impluvium*.

diachronic: delating to, or studying the development of a phenomenon through time. Cf. **synchronic**.

dolium: a large earthenware pot used in bars for food sales.

down pipe: 'a pipe leading downwards; especially a pipe to carry rain-water from a roof to a drain' (*OED* 1989). There are at least two diameters of down pipe from upper storeys in Pompeii. Little research, if any, has been carried out on these features. In this presentation it will be suggested that those with the larger diameter were from upper storey toilets whilst the narrower diameter pipes carried water. This differentiation may help to explain Adam's comment that 'the numerous latrines on the upper floors were evacuated via large pipes made of terracotta, some of them leading to a ditch, others joining up with the roadway' (Adam 1994: 261).

faeces: 'waste material that is discharged from the bowels; excrement' (*OED* 1989).

forica: large toilet with multiple seating.

fullonica: workplace for the processing and cleansing of wool and cloth.

garum: sauce made from rotting fish.

impluvium: the basin in the middle of the *atrium* into which the water fell from the *compluvium*.

insula: island. Term used for a block of buildings within a city (see also **regio**).

lapilli: the small pieces of pumice which made up a high percentage of the fallout from the eruption of 79 CE.

latrine (Latin *latrina*): 'a privy esp. in a camp, barracks, hospital or such' (*OED* 1970). This definition using the word privy, itself with overtones suggestive of an outside lavatory, is not sufficiently tight. The words 'lavatory' or 'toilet' may appear in this work, but the term 'latrine' will be used to refer to a feature with a seating arrangement and a disposal 'chute' which carries, primarily, faeces and/or urine to a sewer or cesspit. The size of the feature may indicate the number of persons who might be accommodated at any one time.

173

manure: 'dung or compost spread over or mixed with soil to fertilise it' (*OED* 1989). The words 'faeces', 'ordure' and 'excrement' will be used in this book to define the solid waste excreted by humans or animals. 'Manure' is the term used to indicate a purpose for this material in cultivation.

nymphaeum: a shrine area within a house, often with a water feature.

opus craticium: a framework of wood within which mortared brick and rubble is packed; the resulting wall could then be plastered. Used particularly for exterior work on upper storeys and for timber framed partitions resting on the floor or on low walls.

peristyle: a central open area in a Roman house surrounded by a colonnade.

pistrinum: a mill.

praetorium: the living quarters of the commander of a fort.

regio: a region. Pompeii was divided into nine regions for analytical purposes by the archaeologist Giuseppe Fiorelli. Each *regio* was subdivided into *insulae* which were also numbered, and these were further subdivided by numbering the entrances into each property.

Roman/Pompeian. Academics write about Italy and the Romans as though the two are synonymous and synchronic, even though they themselves understand that the Romanisation of that part of the world was a gradual process. Other peoples, Greeks, Oscans and Samnites (Strabo *Geography* V.4.8; Descoeudres 1994: 5) built and inhabited Pompeii long before Rome became powerful. Although Pompeii came under the influence of Rome it was a Roman *colonia* only for the 160 years prior to its destruction. In order to avoid confusion, the word 'Pompeian' will be used to cover all aspects of the time period relating to the city of Pompeii, but 'Roman' will be used when discussing broad cultural concepts, unless other derivations are specifically mentioned.

rubbish: see **waste.**

sewer: '(1) an artificial watercourse for draining marshy land and carrying off surface water into a river or the sea; (2) an artificial channel or conduit, usually underground, for carrying off and discharging waste water and the refuse from houses and towns' (*OED* 1970). Research is often complicated by usage of a word which may have more than one meaning. An article entitled 'Roman sewers and sewerage networks – neglected areas of study' (Reimers 1991), might be assumed to be concerned with human excrement. However this particular aspect of effluent disposal is not mentioned; the paper is solely concerned with water drains. Throughout this book the word 'sewer' will be used only to describe a pipe which transmits human effluent. Other outlet pipe systems associated with water systems will be described as 'drains'.

soak-away pit: 'a pit, usually filled with hard-core, into which water or other liquids may flow and from which they may percolate slowly into the surrounding subsoil' (*OED* 1989). A soak-away pit is the feature into which the material is deposited via the toilet. The natural decay of such material, associated especially with a good supply of water, will allow a total seepage of material into the substratum, provided that it is sufficiently permeable. Some confusion may occur with the usage of the term 'soak-away pit'. For example, in the description of the excavations at Cosa there are no mentions of latrines. 'Most of the houses excavated at Cosa have individual soak-away pits for the disposal of waste' (Bruno & Scott 1993: 124). One such pit is described as containing 'a complete wheel-made lamp, a black glaze plate and a fine ware beaker'. Another similar pit contained 'three pre-Arretine plates and one pre-Arretine cup' (Bruno & Scott 1993: 73). Care must be taken in the analysis of waste disposal to make clear the distinction between a soak-away catering for a latrine, such as is the norm in Pompeii, and any other pit into which waste products may be deposited. In this study the term 'cesspit' will be used to define a pit dug for faecal waste. The more modern expression 'septic tank' is defined as 'a tank (associated with a sewage works or with a residence that is not connected to a main sewer) in which the solid portions of sewage are allowed to settle and accumulate and are purified by the action of anaerobic bacteria' (*OED* 1989).

stercus: manure/faeces.

stercorarius: labourer who removed manure/faeces.

synchronic: concerned with events or phenomena occurring at the same period of time. Cf. **diachronic**.

terra sigillata: ceramic ware with a red glaze.

thermopolium: a place where warm food was served.

waste/rubbish

waste: 'refuse matter, unserviceable material remaining over from any process of manufacture. The useless by-products of any industrial process, material or manufactured articles so damaged as to be useless or unsaleable' (*OED* 1989).

rubbish: 'waste or refuse material, debris, litter, rejected and useless material of any kind' (*OED* 1989).

In the context of this discussion, 'waste' is synonymous with 'garbage', 'refuse', 'rubbish', 'debris', 'detritus' and 'litter'. A distinction will be drawn with human waste which will be termed excreta (excrement) or faeces (faecal material). This definition itself is slightly misleading because humans have other waste products such as breath, sweat and flatus. Urine, another human waste product, will be defined separately from faecal excreta.

Bibliography

Ancient works in translation

Athenaeus, *The Deipnosophists*, tr. C.B. Gulick, vol. 5, book 12 (London: Heinemann, 1933).

Celsus, *De Medicina*, tr. W.G. Spencer, Loeb Classical Library 292, 304, 336 (Cambridge, MA: Harvard University Press, 1971).

Cicero, *De Natura Deorum*, tr. H. Rackham, Loeb Classical Library 268 (Cambridge, MA: Harvard University Press, 1933).

CIL = Corpus Inscriptionum Latinarum (Berlin, 1853-).

Columella, *On Agriculture & Trees III*, tr. E.S. Forster & E.H. Heffner, Loeb Classical Library 408 (Cambridge, MA: Harvard University Press, 1955).

Columella, *On Agriculture*, tr. Harrison Boyd Ash, Loeb Classical Library 361 (Cambridge, MA.: Harvard University Press, 2001).

Fontes Iuris Romani Antejustiniani (FIRA), ed. S. Riccobono, J. Baviera, C. Ferrini & V. Arangio-Ruiz, 3 vols (Florence 1941, 1940, 1943).

Frontinus, *The Stratagems: The Aqueducts of Rome*, tr. Charles E. Bennett, Loeb Classical Library 174 (Cambridge, MA: Harvard University Press,1997).

Herodotus, *The History*, tr. D. Grene (Chicago: University of Chicago Press, 1987).

Hesiod, *Works and Days*, tr. G.W. Most, Loeb Classical Library 57 (Cambridge, MA: Harvard University Press, 2007).

Horace, *Satires, Epistles and Poetica* 1999, tr. H.R. Fairclough, Loeb Classical Library 194 (Cambridge, MA: Harvard University Press, 1999).

Juvenal and Persius, tr. G.G. Ramsay, Loeb Classical Library (London: Heinemann, 1918), now superseded by Juvenal and Persius, tr. S.M. Braund, Loeb Classical Library 91 (Cambridge, MA: Harvard University Press, 2004).

Lucretius, *De Rerum Natura*, tr. W.H.D. Rouse, Loeb Classical Library (London: Heinemann, 1924).

Martial, *Epigrams*, tr. D.R. Shackleton Bailey, Loeb Classical Library 94, 95, 480, vols I, II & III (Cambridge, MA: Harvard University Press, 1993).

Petronius, *Satyricon*, tr. M. Heseltine, revised E.H. Warmington, *Apocolocyntosis/Seneca*, Loeb Classical Library (Cambridge, MA: Harvard University Press).

Plautus, *Plays* I, tr. P. Nixon, Loeb Classical Library 60 (London: Heinemann, 1916).

Pliny the Elder, *Natural History*, tr. W.H.S. Jones, Loeb Classical Library 330, 352, 353, 370, 371, 392, 394, 418, 419 (Cambridge, MA: Harvard University Press, 1963).

Pliny the Younger, *Letters*, tr. B. Radice, Loeb Classical Library 59 (Cambridge, MA: Harvard University Press, 1969).

Polybius, *The Rise of the Roman Empire*, tr. I. Scott-Kilvert, Penguin Classics (Harmondsworth: Penguin, 1979).

Scriptores Historiae Augustae, tr. D. Magie, Loeb Classical Library 139 (Cambridge, MA: Harvard University Press, 1967).

Seneca, *Ad Lucilium Epistulae Morales III*, tr. R.M. Gummere, Loeb Classical Library 75 (London: Heinemann, 1925).

Statius, *Silvae – Thebaid I-IV*, tr. D.R. Shackleton Bailey, Loeb Classical Library 206 (Cambridge, MA: Harvard University Press, 2003).

Strabo, *The Geography of Strabo I, II*, tr. H.L. Jones, Loeb Classical Library 49, 50 (Cambridge, MA: Harvard University Press, 1923).

Suetonius, *Lives of the Caesars VIII The Deified Vespasian*, tr. J.C. Rolfe, Loeb Classical Library 31 (Cambridge, MA: Harvard University Press, 1914).

Tacitus, *Annals*, tr. J. Jackson, Loeb Classical Library 249 (Cambridge, MA: Harvard University Press. 1970).

Valerius Maximus, *Memorable Doings and Sayings*, tr. D.R. Shackleton Bailey, Loeb Classical Library 492 (Cambridge, MA: Harvard University Press, 2000).

Varro, *On Agriculture*, tr. W.D. Hooper, rev. Harrison Boyd Ash, Loeb Classical Library 283 (Cambridge, MA: Harvard University Press, 1999).

Varro, *Saturarum Manippearum Fragmenta*, ed. R. Astbury (Leipzig, B.G. Teubner Verlagsgesellschaft, 1985).

Vitruvius, *The Ten Books on Architecture*, tr. Morris Hicky Morgan (New York: Dover Publications, 1960).

Modern references

Abbott, F.F. & Johnson, A.C. (1926) *Municipal Administration in the Roman Empire* (Princeton: Princeton University Press).

Adam, J-P. (1994) *Roman Building: Materials and Techniques* (London: Batsford).

Adams, W.Y. (1985) 'Primis and the "Aethiopian" frontier', *Journal of the American Research Center in Egypt* 20: 95-104.

Alan, V.R., Robertson, A.S., Maxwell, G., Hartley, B.R., Clarke, A.S. (1974) 'The Roman Fort at Cramond. Edinburgh Excavation 1954-1966', *Britannia* 5: 163-224.

Amulree, Lord (1973) 'Hygienic conditions in ancient Rome and modern London', *Medical History* 17: 244-55.

Arthur, P. (1986) 'Problems of the urbanization of Pompeii: excavations 1980-1981', *Antiquaries Journal* 66: 129-44.

Ballu, A. (1911) *Les Ruines de Timgad* (Paris: Neurdein Frères).

Bartosiewicz, L. (2003) 'There's something rotten in the State ...': *Antiquity, European Journal of Archaeology* 6 (2): 175-95.

Berry, James (1921) 'A latrine of Roman Imperial times', *Proceedings of the Royal Society of Medicine, History of Medicine* 14: 17-20.

Berry, J. (1997a) 'The conditions of domestic life in Pompeii in AD 79: a case-study of Houses 11 and 12 Insula 9 Region I', *Papers of the British School at Rome* 65: 103-25 (London: British Academy).

Berry, J. (1997b) Household artefacts: towards a re-interpretation of Roman domestic space', in R. Laurence & A. Wallace-Hadrill (eds) *Domestic Space in the Roman World: Pompeii and Beyond, Journal of Roman Archaeology* Supplementary Series 22: 183-95.

Bodel, J. (2000) 'Dealing with the dead: undertakers, executioners and potter's field in ancient Rome', in V.M. Hope & E. Mardhall (eds) *Death and Disease in the Ancient City* (London: Routledge).

Boersma, J. (1996) 'Private latrines in Ostia: a case study', *Bulletin Antieke Beschaving (BABesch.)* 71: 151-60.

Bourke, J.G. (1891) *Scatological Rites of all Nations* (Washington, DC: W.H. Lowdermilk & Co.).

Boyer, P. (1999) 'The Parasites', in A. Connor & R. Buckley, *Roman and Medieval Occupation in Causeway Lane, Leicester*, Leicester Archaeology Monograph 5: 344-6.

Bradley, M. (2002) ' "It all comes out in the wash": looking harder at the Roman *fullonica*', *Journal of Roman Archaeology* 15: 21-43.

Breeze, D.J. (1971) 'Barburgh Mill', *Current Archaeology* 28: 121-4.

Breeze, D.J. (1984) *The Roman Fort on the Antonine Wall at Bearsden*, Studies in Scottish Antiquity 32-68.

Breton, E. (1855) *Pompeia* (Paris: Baudry).

Brion, M. (1960) *Pompeii and Herculaneum: The Glory and the Grief* (London: Elek).

Brissaud, L. (2003) 'Un vase de foulon sur le site de saint-Romain-en-Galle? Hypothèses et pistes de recherche', in R. Ballet, P. Cordier & N. Dieudonné-Glad (eds) *La Ville et ses déchets dans la monde romain: rebuts et recyclages*, Actes du colloque de Poitiers (19-21 Septembre 2002) (Montagnac: Monique Mergoil).

Browning, I. (1979) *Palmyra* (London: Chatto and Windus).

Browning, I. (1982) *Jerash and the Decapolis* (London: Chatto and Windus).

Bryant, V.M. (1974) 'Prehistoric diet in Southwest Texas: the coprolite evidence', *American Antiquity* 39: 407-20.

Bryant, V.M. & Williams-Dean, G. (1975) 'The coprolites of man', *Scientific American* 232(1): 100-9.

Buckland, P.C. (1976) *The Environmental Evidence from the Church Street Roman Sewer System*, The Archaeology of York 14/1 (London: Council for British Archaeology).

Bull, I.D., Lockheart, M.J., Elhmmali, M.M., Roberts, D.J. & Evershed, R.P. (2002) 'The origin of faeces by means of biomarker detection', *Environmental International* 27: 647-54.

Burn, A.R. (1953) 'Hic breve vivitur', *Past and Present* 4: 2-31.

Cahill, J., Reinhard, K., Tarler, D. & Warnock, P. (1991) 'Scientists examine remains of ancient bathroom', *Biblical Archaeological Review* 27: 64-9.

Callen, E.O. (1969) 'Diet as revealed by coprolites', in D. Brothwell & E. Higgs (eds) *Science in Archaeology*, rev. edn (London: Thames & Hudson).

Callen, E.O. & Cameron, T.W.M. (1960) 'A prehistoric diet revealed in coprolites', *New Scientist* 8.190: 35-40.

Capasso, L. (1998) 'Lice buried under the ashes of Herculaneum', *Lancet* 351: 992.

Capasso, L. (2000) 'Herculaneum victims of the volcanic eruptions of Vesuvius in 79 AD', *Lancet* 356: 1344-6.

Capasso, L. (2002) 'Bacteria in two-millennia-old cheese, and related epizoonoses in Roman populations', *Journal of Infection* 45(2): 122-6.

Chini, P. (1995) 'Forica Romana in Via Garibaldi', *Archaeologia Laziale* 12: 207-12.

Ciaraldi, M. & Richardson, J. (1999) 'Food, ritual and rubbish in the making of Pompeii', in G. Fincham, G. Harrison, R. Holland & L. Revell (eds), *TRAC99: Proceedings of the Ninth Annual Theoretical Roman Conference* (Oxford: Oxbow Books), 74-91.

Ciaraldi, M.R.A. (2001), *Food and Fodder, Religion and Medicine at Pompeii*, PhD thesis, University of Bradford.

Cipolla, C.M. (1992) *Miasmas and Disease: Public Health and the Environment in the Pre-industrial Age*, tr. E. Potter (New Haven and London: Yale University Press).

Clark, P. & Davis, A. (1989) 'The power of dirt: an exploration of secular defilement in Anglo-Canadian culture', *Canadian Review of Sociology and Anthropology* 26(4): 650-73.

Clarke, W. (1831) *Pompeii*, vols I & II, Library of Entertaining Knowledge (London: Charles Knight).

Coppens, E. (2006) 'AA 611 Final Report', unpublished excavation report, Anglo-American Project in Pompeii.

Corbin, A. (1986) *The Foul and the Fragrant: Odor and the French Social Imagination* (Leamington Spa: Berg).

Crouch, D.P. (1993) *Water Management in Ancient Greek Cities* (Oxford: Oxford University Press).

Crump, W.B. & Ghorbal, G. (1935) *History of the Huddersfield Woollen Industry* (Huddersfield: Tolson Memorial Museum Publications handbook).

Dague, R.R. (1972) 'Fundamentals of odor control', *Journal of the Water Pollution Control Federation* 48: 583-94.

Daremberg, C. & Saglio, E. (eds) (1873-1910) *Dictionnaire des antiquités grecques et romaines* (Paris: Hachette).

De Haan, N. (2001) 'Pompeian private baths and the use of water', in A.O. Koloski-Ostrow (ed.) *Water Use and Hydraulics in the Roman City*, AIA Colloquia and Conference Papers 3: 41-7.

De Jorio, A. (1820) *Ricerche sul tempio di Serapide in Pozzuoli* (Naples).

Descoeudres, J-P. (1994) *Pompeii Revisited: The Life and Death of a Roman Town* (Sydney: Meditarch).

Descoeudres, J-P. & Sear, F. (1987) 'The Australian expedition to Pompeii', *Rivisti di Studi Pompeiani* 1: 11-36.

Dickson, C. & Dickson, J. (2000) 'Roman invasions: foreign foodstuffs, weeds and medicines', in C. Dickson & J. Dickson, *Plants and People in Ancient Scotland* (Stroud: Tempus), 114-27.

Dickson, J.H. (1979) 'Exotic food and drink in ancient Scotland', *Glasgow Naturalist* 19 (6): 437-42.

Dimbleby, G.W. (2002) 'Pollen analysis of soil samples from the AD 79 level. Pompeii, Oplontis and Boscoreale', in W.F. Jashemski & F.G. Meyer (eds) *The Natural History of Pompeii* (Cambridge: Cambridge University Press), 181-9.

Dixon, D.M. (1972) 'Population, pollution, and health in ancient Egypt', in *Population and Pollution: Proceedings of the Eighth Annual Symposium of the Eugenics Society 1971* (London: Academic Press), 29-36.

Dixon, D.M. (1989) 'A note on some scavengers of ancient Egypt', *World Archaeology* 21(2): 193-97.

Dodge, H. (2000) ' "Greater than the Pyramids": the water supply of Ancient Rome', in J. Coulston & H. Dodge (eds) *Ancient Rome: The Archaeology of the Ancient City:* (Oxford: Oxford University School of Archaeology Monograph 54), 166-209.

Douglas, M. (1966) *Purity and Danger: An Analysis of Concepts of Pollution and Taboo* (London: Routledge & Kegan Paul).

Dubbin, A.M. (2003) *Analysis of Faecal Deposits from Pompeii, Italy: A New Source of Evidence for Ancient Diet and Urban Ecology*, unpublished M.Sc. dissertation, University of Bradford.

Dunbabin, K.M.D. (1978) *The Mosaics of North Africa* (Oxford: Clarendon Press).

Dunbabin, K.M.D. (1989) 'Baiarum grata voluptas: pleasures and dangers of the baths', *Proceedings of the British School at Rome* 57: 6-46 (London: British Academy).

Dyer, Thomas H. (1867) *Pompeii: Its History, Buildings, and Antiquities* (London: Bell and Daldy).

Eschebach, H. (1979) *Die Stabianer Thermen in Pompeji*, Deutches Archäologisches Institut, Band 13 (Berlin: De Gruyter).

Bibliography

Fagan, G.G. (2002) 'Hygienic conditions in Roman public baths', in G.C.M. Jansen (ed.) *Cura Aquarum in Sicilia* (Leiden: Stichting BABesch.), 281-7.

Faulkner, C.T. (1991) 'Prehistoric diet and parasitic infection in Tennessee: evidence from the analysis of desiccated human paleofeces', *American Antiquity* 56(4): 687-700, repr. in W.F. Jashemski & F.G. Meyer (eds) (2002) *The Natural History of Pompeii* (Cambridge: Cambridge University Press), 182-216.

Field, R. (1998) *Geometric Patterns from Roman Mosaics* (Diss: Tarquin Publications).

Fino, L. (2006) *Herculaneum and Pompeii in the 18th and 19th Centuries* (Naples: Grimaldi).

[Fiorelli] Pappalardo, U. (2001) *La Descrizione di Pompei per Guiseppe Fiorelli (1875)* (Napoli: Massa Editore).

Franklin, J.L. Jr. (1991) 'Literacy and the parietal inscriptions of Pompeii', in J.H. Humphrey (ed.) *Literacy in the Roman World*, *Journal of Roman Archaeology* Supplementary Series 3.

Frere, S. (1967) *Britannia: A History of Roman Britain* (London: Book Club Associates).

Frere, S. et al. (1977) 'Roman Britain in 1976', *Britannia* 8: 355-425.

Fox, A. et al. (1972) 'The Roman Fort at Nanstallon, Cornwall', *Britannia* 3: 56-111.

Garrison, F.A. (1929) 'The history of drainage, irrigation, sewage disposal and water supply', *Bulletin of New York Academy of Medicine* 5: 887-938.

Gell, Sir William & Gandy, John P. (1852) *Pompeiana* (London: Henry G. Bohn).

Goldwater, A. (2002) *Military Latrines in Roman Britain*, MA dissertation. University of Nottingham.

Germain, S. (1969) *Les mosaïques de Timgad* (Aris Éditions, CNRS).

Goudineau, C. et al. (1979) *Les Fouilles de la Maison au Dauphin* (Paris: Éditions du Centre National de la Recherche Scientifique).

Grahame, M. (2000) *Reading Space: Social Interaction and Identity in the Houses of Roman Pompeii*, BAR International Series 886.

Greig, J. (1982) 'Gardrobes, sewers, cesspits and latrines', *Current Archaeology* 85: 49-52.

Grüger, E. (2002) 'Pollen analysis of soil samples from the AD 79 level: Pompeii, Oplontis and Boscoreale', in W.F. Jashemski & F.G. Meyer (eds) *The Natural History of Pompeii* (Cambridge: Cambridge University Press), 182-216.

Gusman, P. (c. 1900) *Une ville antique sous les cendres: Pompéi* (Paris: Société Française d'Éditions d'Art).

Hales, S. (2003) *The Roman House and Social Identity* (Cambridge: Cambridge University Press).

Halifax, W. (1695) *Report on a Voyage to Palmyra* (London: Philosophical Transactions of the Royal Society).

Hall, A.R. & Kenward, H.K. (1990) *Environmental Evidence from the Colonia*, The Archaeology of York 14/6 (London: Council for British Archaeology).

Hall, A.R., Kenward, H.K., Williams, D. & Greig, J.R.A. (1983) *Environment and Living Conditions at Two Anglo-Scandinavian Sites*, The Archaeology of York 14/4 (London: Council for British Archaeology).

Hall, E.T. (1968) 'Proxemics', *Current Anthropology* 9(2-3): 83-95.

Hallé, J-N. (1787) *Recherches sur la nature et les effets du méphitisme des fosses d'aisances* (Paris).

Halstead, P., Hodder, I. & Jones, G. (1978) 'Behavioural archaeology and refuse patterns: a case study', *Norwegian Archaeological* Review II(1): 118-31.

Harris, W.V. (1999) 'Demography, geography and the sources of Roman slaves', *Journal of Roman Studies* 89: 62-75.

181

Haverfield, F. (1913) *Ancient Town Planning* (Oxford: Clarendon Press).

Hayden, B. & Cannon, A. (1983) 'Where the garbage goes: refuse disposal in the Maya highlands', *Journal of Anthropological Archaeology* 2: 117-63.

Herbert, D.T. & Thomas, C.J. (1997) *Cities in Space: City as Place* (London: David Fulton).

Hesse, B. & Wapnish, P. (1985) *Animal Bone Archaeology from Objectives to Analysis* (Washington: Taraxacum Press).

Hill, J.D. (1996) 'The identification of ritual deposits of animal bones: a general perspective from a specific study of "special animal deposits" from the southern English Iron Age', in S. Anderson & K. Boyle (eds) *Ritual Treatment of Human and Animal Remains: Proceedings of the First Meeting of the Osteoarchaeological Research Group held in Cambridge on 8th October 1994* (Oxford: Oxbow Books), 17-32.

Hobson, J.B. (1998) *AA110 Final Report*, unpublished excavation report, Anglo-American Project in Pompeii.

Hobson, J.B. (2002) *AA185 Final Report*, unpublished excavation report, Anglo-American Project in Pompeii.

Hobson, J.B. (2004a) *AA400 Final Report*, unpublished excavation report, Anglo-American Project in Pompeii.

Hodge, A. Trevor (1992) *Roman Aqueducts and Water Supply* (London: Duckworth).

Holden, T.G. (1991) 'Evidence of prehistoric diet from northern Chile: coprolites, gut contents and flotation samples from the Tulán Quebrada', *World Archaeology* 22(3): 320-31.

Holmes, N. (1977) 'Cramond', *Current Archaeology* 59: 378-81.

Hopkins, K. (1966) 'On the probable age structure of the Roman population', *Population Studies* 20 (2): 245-64.

Horne, John Fletcher (1895) *The Buried Cities of Vesuvius, Herculaneum and Pompeii* (London: Hazell, Watson and Viney).

Isaac, P.C.G. (1958) 'Roman public-works engineering', *University of Durham King's College Department of Civil Engineering Bulletin* 13.

Jackson, R. (1988) *Doctors and Diseases in the Roman Empire* (London: British Museum Publications).

Jansen, G.C.M. (1992) 'Water systems and sanitation in the Houses of Herculaneum', *Mededelingen van het Nederlands Institut te Rome* 50: 145-66.

Jansen, G.C.M. (1993) 'Paintings in Roman toilets', in E.M. Moormann (ed.) *Functional and Spatial Analysis of Wall Painting* (Leiden: Stichting BABesch.), 29-33.

Jansen, G.C.M. (1994) 'Sewers and tap water as urban innovations at Herculaneum', in *XIVè Congrés Internacional d'Arqueologia Clàssica* (Tarragona), 218-20.

Jansen, G.C.M. (1997) 'Private toilets in Pompeii: appearance and operation', in S.E. Bon & R. Jones (eds) *Sequence and Space in Pompeii*, Oxbow Monograph 77 (Oxford: Oxbow Books), 121-34.

Jansen, G.C.M. (2000a) 'Systems for the disposal of waste and excreta in Roman cities: the situation in Pompeii, Herculaneum and Ostia', in X.D. Raventós & J-A Remolà (eds) *Sordes Urbis: La Eliminación de Residuos en le Ciudad Romana* (Rome: L'Erma di Bretschneider), 37-49.

Jansen, G.C.M. (2000b) 'Studying Roman hygiene: the battle between the "optimists" and the "pessimists"', in G.C.M. Jansen (ed.) *Cura Aquarum in Sicilia* (Leiden: Stichting BABesch.), 275-9.

Jansen, G.C.M. (2001) 'Water pipe systems in the houses of Pompeii: distribution

Bibliography

and use', in A.O. Koloski-Ostrow (ed.) *Water Use and Hydraulics in the Roman City*, AIA Colloquia and Conference Papers 3: 27-40.

Jansen, G.C.M. (2002) *Water in de Romeinse stad: Pompeji – Herculaneum – Ostia*, Doctoral thesis, University of Nijmegen (Maastricht: Peeters).

Jansen, G.C.M. (2003) 'Social distinctions and issues of privacy in the toilets of Hadrian's Villa', *Journal of Roman Archaeology* 16: 137-52.

Jashemski, W.F. (1979) *The Gardens of Pompeii: Herculaneum and the Villas Destroyed by Vesuvius* (New York: Caratzas Bros.).

Johnson, A. (1983) *Roman Forts* (London: A.&C. Black).

Johnson, A.C., Coleman-Norton, P.R. & Bourne, F.C. (1961) *Ancient Roman Statutes* (Austin: University of Texas Press).

Jones, A.K.G. (1985) 'Trichurid ova in archaeological deposits: their value as indicators of ancient faeces', in N.R.J. Fieller, D.D. Gilbertson & N.G.A. Ralph (eds) *Palaeobiological Investigations: Research Design, Methods and Data Analysis*, BAR International Series 266: 105-17.

Jones, A.K.G. (1992) 'Coprolites and faecal material in archaeological deposits: a methodological approach', in M. Bernardi (ed.) *Archeologia del Passagio* (Firenze), 287-301.

Jones, R. (ed.) *Sequence and Space in Pompeii*, Oxbow Monograph 77 (Oxford: Oxbow Books), 121-34.

Jones, R.F.J. & Robinson, D.J. (2005) 'The economic development of the commercial triangle (VI.1.14-18, 20-21)', in P.G. Guzzo & M.P. Guidobaldi (eds) *Nuove Recherche Archeologiche a Pompei ed Ercolano*, Studi della Soprintendenza Archeologica di Pompei 10 (Napoli: Electa), 270-7.

Kamash, Z. (2006) *Water Supply and Management in the Near East, 63 BC-AD 636*, unpublished DPhil. thesis, University of Oxford.

Kenward, H.K., Hall, A.R. & Jones, A.K.G. (1986) *Environmental Evidence from a Roman Well and Anglian Pits in the Legionary Fortress*, The Archaeology of York 14/5 (London: Council for British Archaeology).

Kenward, H.K. & Hall, A.R. (1995) *Biological Evidence from Anglo-Scandinavian Deposits at 16-22 Coppergate*, The Archaeology of York 14/7 (London: Council for British Archaeology).

Kipling, R. (1919) 'Natural Theology', in *The Years Between* (London: Methuen), 121-4.

Kira, A. (1970) 'Privacy and the bathroom', in H.M. Proshansky, W.H. Ittelson & L.G. Rivlin (eds), *Environmental Psychology: Man and his Physical Setting* (New York: Holt, Rinehart & Winston), 269-75.

Knörzer, K-H. (1984) 'Aussagemögligkeiten von paläoethnobotanischen Latrinenuntersuchungen [The prospects of the palaeoethnobotanical examination of cesspits]', in W. Van Zeist & W.A. Casparia (eds) *Plant Remains and Ancient Man* (Rotterdam: Balkane), 331-8.

Koloski-Ostrow, A.O. (1996) 'Finding social meaning in the public latrines of Pompeii', in N. de Haan & G.C.M. Jansen (eds) *Cura Aquarum in Campania: Proceedings of the Ninth International Congress on the History of Water Management and Hydraulic Engineering in the Mediterranean Region* (Leiden: Stichting BABesch.), 79-86.

Koloski-Ostrow, A.O. (2000) '*Cacator cave malum:* the subject and object of Roman public latrines in Italy during the first centuries BC and AD', in G.C.M. Jansen (ed.) *Cura Aquarum in Sicilia* (Leiden: Stichting BABesch.), 289-95.

Koloski-Ostrow, A.O. (ed.) (2001) *Water Use and Hydraulics in the Roman City*, AIA Colloquia and Conference Papers 3.

Kuijper, W.J. & Turner, H. (1992) 'Diet of a Roman centurion at Alphen aan den Rijn, The Netherlands, in the first century AD', *Review of Palaeobotany and Palynology* 73: 187-204.

Kwawe, D.B. (1995) 'Culture of waste handling: experience of a rural community', *Journal of Asian and African studies* 30(1-2): 53-67.

Lambton, L. (1978) *Temples of Convenience* (London: Gordon Fraser).

Lambton, L. (1983) *Chambers of Delight* (London: Gordon Fraser).

Lanciani, R. (1873) *Bullettino della Commissione Archeologica Communale di Roma* 3: 242-54.

Lanciani, R. (1897) *The Ruins and Excavations of Ancient Rome* (London: Macmillan & Co.).

Leach, E.R. (1971) 'Anthropological aspects: conclusion', in *Population and Pollution: Proceedings of the Eighth Annual Symposium of the Eugenics Society 1971* (London: Academic Press), 37-40.

Leon, H.J. (1941) 'Sulphur for broken glass', *Transactions and Proceedings of the American Philological Association* 72: 233-6.

Liebeschuetz, W. (2000) 'Rubbish disposal in Greek and Roman cities' in X.D. Raventós & J-A. Remolà (eds) *Sordes Urbis: La Eliminación de Residuos en le Ciudad Romana* (Rome: L'Erma di Bretschneider), 51-61.

Ling, R. (1997) *The Insula of the Menander at Pompeii*, vol. 1: *The Structures* (Oxford: Clarendon Press).

Linskens, H.F. & Jorde, W. (1997) 'Pollen as food and medicine – a review', *Economic Botany* 51(1): 78-86.

Love, M. (2007) *Analysis of Calcareous Deposits from the Down Pipes of First Century Pompeii*, unpublished dissertation, University of Bradford.

MacDonald, G. (1902) 'The Roman wall in Scotland', *Proceedings of the Society of Antiquaries of Scotland* 37: 271-346.

Maiuri, A. (1954) *Herculaneum*, Guide Books to the Museums, Galleries and Monuments of Italy no. 53 (Rome: Istituto Poligrafico dello Stato).

Maltby, M. (1994) 'The meat supply in Roman Dorchester and Winchester', in A.R. Hall & H. Kenward (eds) *Urban-rural Connexions: Perspectives from Environmental Archaeology*, Oxbow Monograph 47 (Oxford: Oxbow Books), 85-102.

Martin, A.T. & Ashby, T. (1901) 'Excavations at Caerwent, on the site of Venta Silurum in 1899 and 1900', *Archaeologia* XVII.

Martin, L. & Russell, N. (2000) 'Trashing rubbish', in I. Hodder (ed.) *Towards Reflexive Method in Archaeology: The Example at Çatalhöyük*, British Institute of Archaeology at Ankara Monograph 28 (McDonald Institute Monographs), 57-69.

Martin, P.S. & Sharrock, F.W. (1964) 'Pollen analysis of prehistoric human feces: a new approach to ethnobotany', *American Antiquity* 30(2): 168-80.

Mau, A. (1902). *Pompeii: Its Life and Art*, tr. W. Kelsey (New York: Macmillan).

Mygind, H. (1921) 'Hygienische Verhältisse im alten Pompeji', *Janus* 25: 251-383.

Nash-Williams, V.E. (1931) 'The Roman legionary fortress at Caerleon in Monmouthshire: report on the excavations carried out in the Prysg Field 1927-9', *Archaeologia Cambrensis* 86.

Neudecker, R. (1994) *Der Pracht die Latrine* (Munchen: Verlag Dr. Friedrich Pfeil).

Nielsen, I. (1990a) *Thermae et balnea. I. Text* (Aarhus: Aarhus University Press).

Nielsen, I. & Schiøler, T. (1980) 'The water system in the Baths of Mithras in Ostia', *Analecta Romana* 9: 149-59.

Nutton, V. (1983) 'The seeds of disease: an explanation of contagion and infection from the Greeks to the Renaissance', *Medical History* 27: 1-34.

Bibliography

Nutton, V. (1985) 'The drug trade in antiquity', *Journal of the Royal Society of Medicine* 78: 138-45.

Packer, J. (1978) 'Inns at Pompei', *Cronache Pompeianae* 4: 5-53.

Panciera, S. (2000) 'Nettezza urbana a Roma: organizzazione e responsabili', in X.D. Raventós & J-A. Remolà (eds) *Sordes Urbis: La Eliminación de Residuos en le Ciudad Romana* (Roma: L'Erma di Bretschneider), 99-105.

Parkin, T. (1992) *Demography and Roman Society* (Baltimore: Johns Hopkins University Press).

Parslow, C. (2000) 'The hydraulic system in the *balneum venerium et nongentum* of the Praedia Iuliae Felicis in Pompeii', in G.C.M. Jansen (ed.) *Cura Aquarum in Sicilia* (Leiden: Stichting BABesch.), 201-9.

Pike, A.W. & Biddle, M. (1966) 'Parasite eggs in medieval Winchester', *Antiquity* 40: 293-6.

Pirson, F. (1999) *Mietwohnungen in Pompeji und Herculaneum* (München: Dr Friedrich Pfeil).

Porter, R. (ed.) (1996) *The Cambridge Illustrated History of Medicine* (Cambridge: Cambridge University Press).

Price, J. & Cool, H.E.M. (1991) 'The evidence for the production of glass in Roman Britain', in D. Foy & G. Sennequier (eds) *Ateliers de Verriers de l'Antiquité à la Période Pré-Industrielle*, Association Française pour l'Archéologie du Verre, Actes des 4èmes Rencontres, Rouen 1989, 23-9.

Rathje, W. & Murphy, C. (1992) *Rubbish! The Archaeology of Garbage* (Harper Perennial).

Redknap, M. (1976a) 'A lavatory seat from Neatham, Hampshire', *Britannia* 7: 287-8.

Redknap, M. (1976b) *Roman Latrines and Urban Sanitation: Current Work and Problems*, unpublished dissertation, University College London.

Reimers, P. (1991) 'Roman sewers and sewerage networks – neglected areas of study', *Munuscula Romana*, 111-16.

Reinhard, K.J., Hamilton, D.R. & Hevly, R.H. (1991) 'Use of pollen concentration in palaeopharmacology', *Journal of Ethnobiology* 11(1): 117-32.

Richardson, J., Thompson, G. & Genovese, A. (1997) 'New directions in economic and environmental research at Pompeii', in S.E. Bon & R. Jones (eds) *Sequence and Space in Pompeii*, Oxbow Monograph 77 (Oxford: Oxbow Books), 88-101.

Robinson, O.F. (1992) *Ancient Rome: City Planning and Administration* (London and New York: Routledge).

Rodriquez Almeida, E. (2002) 'Roma, una città self cleaning?', in X.D. Raventós & J-A. Remolà (eds) *Sordes Urbis: La Eliminación de Residuos en le Ciudad Romana* (Rome: L'Erma di Bretschneider), 123-7.

Rosen, G. (1993) *A History of Public Health: Expanded Version* (Baltimore: Johns Hopkins University Press).

Sabine, E.L. (1934) 'Latrines and cesspools in medieval London', *Speculum* 9: 303-21.

Sabine, E.L. (1970) 'City cleaning in Medieval London', *Speculum* 12: 19-43.

Samuels, R. (1965) 'Parasitological study of long-dried fecal samples', *Memoirs of the Society of American Archaeology* 175-9.

Scarborough, J. (1980) 'Roman medicine and public health', in S. Susoni-shi (ed.), *Public Health: Proceedings of the 5th International Symposium on the Comparative History of Medicine – East and West, Oct 26th-Nov 1st 1980* (Tokyo), 33-73.

Scheidel, W. (2003) 'Germs for Rome' in C. Edwards & G. Woolf (eds) *Rome the Cosmopolis* (Cambridge: Cambridge University Press), 158-76.

Schiffer, M.B. (1985) 'Is there a Pompeii premise in archaeology?', *Journal of Anthropological Research* 1:18-41.

Scobie, A. (1986) 'Slums, sanitation, and mortality in the Roman world', *Klio* 68: 399-433.

Sear, F. (1994) 'Water supply to the House of the Painted Capitals', in J-P. Descoeudres (ed.), *Pompeii Revisited* (Sydney: Meditarch), 100-2.

Sear, F. (2004) 'Cisterns, drainage and lavatories in Pompeian Houses, Casa del Granduca', *Proceedings of the British School at Rome* 72: 125-66.

Shelton, Jo-Ann (1998) *As the Romans Did* (Oxford: Oxford University Press).

Simpson, F.G. (1976) *Watermills and Military Works on Hadrian's Wall: Excavations in Northumberland 1907-1913* (Kendal: Titus Wilson & Son).

Sogliano, A. (1900) 'Pompei – relazione degli scavi eseguiti durante il mese di novembre 1900', *Notizie degli scavi 1900*, 584-603.

Tanzer, H. (1939) *The Common People of Pompeii: A Study of the Graffiti* (Baltimore: Johns Hopkins University Press).

Taylor, E.L. (1955) 'Parasitic helminths in mediaeval remains', *Veterinary Record* 67 (912): 216-18.

Thédenat, H. (1910) *Pompei* (Librairie Paris: Renouard).

Van Dam, S. & Versloot, A. (1995) 'Antiekgemak. Sanitaire voorzieningen in Ostia Antica', *Spiegel Historiael* 30(1): 12-15.

Watson, G.R. (1983) *The Roman Soldier* (London: Thames & Hudson).

Whitwell, J.B. (1976) *The Church Street Sewer and an Adjacent Building*, The Archaeology of York 3/1 (London: Council for British Archaeology).

Wilson, A. (2000) 'Drainage and sanitation', in O. Wikander (ed.) *Handbook of Ancient Water Technology* (Leiden: Brill), vol. 2: 141-79.

Wilson, A. (2002) 'Detritus, disease and death in the city', *Journal of Roman Archaeology* 15: 479-84.

Wilson, B. (1989) 'Fresh and old table refuse: the recognition and location of domestic activity at archaeological sites in the Upper Thames Valley, England', *Archaeozoologia* 3 (1.2): 237-62.

Wilson, R.J.A. (2002) *A Guide to the Roman Remains in Britain* (London: Constable).

Wood, N. (1996) *La Casa del Poeta Tragico/ The House of the Tragic Poet: A Reconstruction* (London: Nicholas Wood).

Wright, L. (1960) *Clean and Decent: The Fascinating History of the Bathroom & the Water Closet* (London: Routledge & Kegan Paul).

Young, B.H. (1910) *The Prehistoric Men of Kentucky*, Filson Club Publications no. 25.

Young, R.L. (1997) *Upstairs at Pompeii*, unpublished MPhil thesis, University of Bradford.

Zanker, P. (1998) *Pompeii: Public and Private Life*, tr. D.L. Schneider (Cambridge, MA: Harvard University Press).

Index of Places